Lady With Power
Dominate Your Fears to Execute Your Vision

Okema Watson

LADY WITH POWER. Copyright © 2022. Okema Watson. All Rights Reserved.

Printed in the United States of America.

No part of this book may be reproduced or transmitted in any or by any means, electronic or mechanical-including scanning, photocopying, recording or by any information storage and retrieval system—whole or in part—without permission in writing from the publisher or author.

Published by

DAYELight
PUBLISHERS

ISBN: 978-1-958443-17-0 (paperback)

To my mother, Manzella Vivene Watson, and my grandmothers, Louise Elizabeth Clarke and Una Rosealee Watson, who were the first ladies to show me just how powerful women can be.

Acknowledgements

To the Creator of my vision and my constant companion—my heavenly Father, without whom this book would still be in the "things to do" section of my mind—I give the highest honour, praise and gratitude.

I am eternally grateful to my biggest supporter and amazing sister, Oksana Watson, for providing endless words of encouragement throughout the process.

I would also like to recognize the invaluable assistance of my publisher, Crystal Daye, and the entire team at DayeLight Publishers. Thank you for helping me to bring this vision to life.

To my family and friends who shared their support through prayer and advise, thank you.

And to you, **Lady With Power**, thank you for trusting me to provide insight as you invest in your dreams and embark on your own journey to execute your vision. May God's will be done in your life.

Table of Contents

Acknowledgements v

Introduction: Your Highest Self 9

The Vessel of Power 13

Purposed for Power 27

The Power of God 41

The Power of Peace 55

The Power of Prayer 69

The Power of Faith 81

The Power of Preparation 91

The Power of Fear 101

The Power of Depression 113

The Power of Unforgiveness 123

Power Lies in the Now 135

Notes 147

About the Author 151

INTRODUCTION:

Your Highest Self

Visualize your highest self and start showing up as her.

I know we're just getting started but right off the bat I want to challenge you to live out the rest of your days on earth with one word in mind, *elevation*. God wants to take you to higher territories in this season, and I know you are not about to allow your fears to rob you of the promises of your Father. The visions, dreams, and ideas that have been waking you up at night need to be released into the world, and despite what the enemy might be telling you, despite the fears, doubts, or insecurities that you might be facing, you actually do have the power to release them. You definitely have the power to execute your vision.

If you are in a job that you have come to realize is no longer fulfilling, then make a plan and change it! If you have a book that you want to write, write it! If you want to go back to school, then do it! If you want to start a podcast, start it! If your desire is to book a ticket to the one place that you have always wanted to visit in search of adventure, then book it! If you have an idea for a business that you want to pursue, then pursue it! If you see a need in your community that you urgently want to address, then address it! Even if you have already done all of this and you still have a desire to achieve more and go higher in your life, then give yourself the permission to go as high as you dare to go. There really doesn't have to be any other reason for wanting to go higher than the very desire you have to challenge yourself, and to leave this earth with the knowledge that you gave everything you could to bring your vision to life. Despite what society has deemed as successful, define what your highest self looks like to you and do everything you can, while you have the opportunity, to reach that level.

The current state of the world, your challenging circumstances, your fears and insecurities, and the things you currently think you lack are no match for the power you possess as you embark on your quest for elevation. Regardless of what you may or may not be going through, this is the time to execute that vision. You still have time; it's not too late, you have not missed all the chances to be the woman you want to be, and your vision is not too ridiculous to pursue.

Despite what might be happening with your finances, your family, your mental health or the state of the world, God knew that this would have been your season to finally step out of your comfort zone and work on achieving those dreams of yours. So rest assured, you'll be provided for. All you have to do is take the first step. Don't allow words such as "logical" and "realistic" to force you into thinking that you are just an ordinary woman who can never show up the way you have envisioned.

In fact, without placing any limitations on what you come up with, just allow yourself to think about what this higher version of you would look like.

1. What would you be doing on a daily basis?
2. Why would you be doing what you envision yourself doing, and how much would you be getting paid to do it?

3. What would you be known for?
4. What are some of the characteristics that you possess?
5. How do you look and feel as your highest self?
6. Do you spend all your time building just yourself or do you give your time to assist with the development of others?

Your Vision Is God's Vision For You

The wonderful ideas you have for your life are not just random thoughts. You may think that these are silly dreams, but they are actually the plans God have in mind and want to set in motion for you. If you are not clear on the answers to the previous questions, then you can seek clarity. Who better to help you with visualizing your highest self than the one who is already the highest of all things created? If you were able to vividly put everything into perspective, then, the next step is to actively work on living as you've imagined.

God has already designed your path to success, so your job is to make sure you release every vision, idea and talent that He has placed on the inside of you. His design, your ideas, and your willingness to act on these ideas are the perfect ingredients for a life of abundance and fulfillment.

It is not that Simple

Once you begin to open up to all the possibilities that life has to offer, it might become easier to envision yourself living beyond the boundaries that once confined you. So the process of actually visualizing your highest self is the easy part; showing up is where things can get a bit more complicated. Unfortunately, when you make the decision to step out of your comfort zone and strive to become more than you originally thought you could be, there are a few opposing forces that may rise up to thwart your efforts. Past failures, negative intrusive thoughts, insecurities, doubts and fears are some of the things that will be activated when you start to dream big, and the main intent of these forces is to destroy your vision.

At this point, you may become discouraged, confused, and drained as you grapple with the desire to work on your goals and the thoughts that you are not good enough to achieve them. On one hand, you may feel capable of starting your business, and on the other hand, you struggle with the fear of failing and the desire to give up because of these fears.

The level at which you desire to live will require a great power that will help you to fight against the forces that just don't want you to accomplish your mission. The good news is that when you were born, you were given the capacity to receive and release this power so you already have what it takes to demolish every opposing power that stands in the way of you showing up the way God intended. Your fears, doubts, and insecurities can be dominated by the power of the Holy Spirit who dwells in you.

The Vessel of Power

But if the Spirit of Him who raised Jesus from the dead dwells in you, He who raised Christ from the dead will also give life to your mortal body through His Spirit who dwells in you.
Romans 8:11 (KJV)

The same power that raised Christ from the dead lives in you. Just allow yourself to think about that for a minute. As you begin to meditate on the fact that you are walking around with resurrection power on the inside of you, you may experience some doubt, and believe me when I tell you that I understand completely. You may be thinking, "Sure, I have certain abilities that have assisted me to accomplish a few things in life, but that's about as far as my potential can get" or maybe your thoughts are more along the lines of "After all the times I have failed in the past and all the mistakes that I have made, there is no way I have that much power."

Regardless of everything that may be against you, the power that dwells inside you can propel you into motion and can in fact give you the strength you need to change your life. Likewise, if you have achieved all that you wanted and still feel the need to go further in life, then the limitless nature of this power can take you where you need to go.

Romans 8 tells us that once we dedicate our lives to living in accordance with the will of God, we will receive His Spirit. Once received, His Spirit will live within us, and we will be gifted with God's resurrecting power; real, everlasting power. This kind of power cannot be destroyed; this power was here before the earth was formed and will be here long after you and I are gone. This power can give life to any situation that appears dead and can heal sicknesses that have physicians scratching their heads in confusion. All proclamations regarding death and defeat are nullified in the presence of this power. This power is key to the maintenance of your faith walk. It will allow you to see through the deceptions of the enemy, recognize your strength and help you move towards achieving your goals. This is the power that you possess.

The power of God can change hearts, open doors that need to be opened, and close those that need to be closed in the physical and spiritual realms. This is a power that protects and provides in times of war, disease, and scarcity. It is the kind that can provide knowledge and wisdom when you are confused, forgiveness when you mess up, and hope when you feel discouraged. Since this power is living in you, then you are able to do far more in life than you can even begin to imagine.

So, if all of this is true, then why do we fail in life? Why is it that sometimes at night tears flow for reasons we cannot seem to find and leave us feeling useless, worthless, and unimportant? Why do we get paralyzed by fear, being unable to move forward with the plans that we map out for our lives?

Well, for every good thing that the Lord prepares for His people, the enemy prepares the opposite. God's power was created to give life to your body and help you to walk upright and confident in the pursuit of your dreams, and the enemy has his own set of powers that were created to kill, steal and destroy everything that you hope to accomplish (see John 10:10). Fear is one of these powers and just as the power of God can dwell in you, the enemy can also find ways for his opposing power to enter your space, impact the way you feel and influence the things you do. For instance, when thoughts of past failures and mistakes flood your mind, you might start to become fearful of repeating these mistakes and being ridiculed by others, so you may end up abandoning all your plans. These thoughts may also cause you to believe that while God's power might be available to everyone else, you are not worthy enough to receive it, and just like that, you're back to ignoring the desires of your heart.

While it can be difficult to completely prevent the enemy's powers from entering your space, you can prevent them from controlling your life. You might have two sets of forces at work in you, but the ones that are nurtured and encouraged are the ones that will grow. Likewise, the ones that you actively try to repel are the ones that eventually become so weak that they no longer play a dominant role in the way you live your life.

The power of God is a mighty challenger against the power of the enemy, and with this power living in you, your determination will ultimately lead to the eviction of everything that threatens your vision. Maybe your life has been so problematic, filled with so much disappointment that now you have just decided to give up and forget about the vision that God gave you. It could also be that your fears are so great that you no longer believe in yourself, causing you to dismiss any idea of activating your vision. Or maybe thoughts of your past mistakes, along with the fear of rejection and failure are making it very hard for you to move forward with your plans.

A powerful woman is not a perfect woman. A woman who walks with the power of God within her doesn't lead a perfect life. God doesn't require perfection in order to give you His power, and receiving His power doesn't mean your life will be without mistakes, fear or even failed endeavours. However, you'll be able to push past all the imperfections, overpower the grip that fear has on your decisions and move towards your goals once you tap into the power of the Holy Spirit.

Once you acknowledge the power of God in you, you'll understand that you really do have what it takes to live the life you want, and even though the enemy uses fear to try and hinder your movements, you do possess the ability to implement your plans and achieve your goals. Okay, fine, you made some mistakes in the past; we all have, but now that you have this desire to make your mark on the earth, you have every right to try and do just that.

Spiritual Oxygen

The Bible teaches that there is one true God who exists as three separate bodies; God, the Father, who created heaven and earth, God, the Son, who came to earth, took on all our sins and died so that we may live, and God, the Holy Spirit, the indwelling force who is our spiritual oxygen needed to supply us with the power and energy to stay alive in Christ. Think of it as the three states of water; under certain circumstances water can become ice, liquid or vapour. Throughout history, our heavenly Father has taken the form of exactly what His people need. Sis, if its power you need in order to bring your vision to life, God can be that for you.

When you accept Jesus as your Lord and Saviour, you are given a new life and you are introduced to new things through Him. Just as you trust that the oxygen you need to stay alive on this earth will be there to keep you going, you can trust that the Holy Spirit within you can give power to your body and provide the energy you need to fight against the powers of the enemy.

Our body needs oxygen in order to build new tissue, convert food to energy, help in the reproduction process, and so many other processes that are essential for our survival. Before you were born, your oxygen supply came directly from your mother. You experienced everything through her up until the point when you entered the world for the first time and could start to breathe on your own.

Having an encounter with the Holy Spirit is like finally being able to breathe on your own for the first time. It is life-changing. It's like you were experiencing life at fifty percent capacity only to now be experiencing a hundred percent functionality. It is a burst of energy; refreshing, renewing, and invigorating. God, the Father, is not just a distant power outside of you, He is now able to work from within and transform you into becoming the woman who is capable of dominating fear.

In order to fully utilize the power of the Holy Spirit, you'll need to allow Him access. The minute the baby takes her own breath, her own life truly begins; no more second hand oxygen. It's time for you to start experiencing your life at maximum capacity. It's now your turn to live with power.

Matthew 10:1 says: *And when he had called unto him his twelve disciples, he gave them power against unclean spirits, to cast them out, and to heal all manner of sickness and all manner of disease. (KJV).*

Then when you go to Acts 2:2-4, this is after Jesus ascended into heaven, it says: *And suddenly there came a sound from heaven as of a rushing mighty wind, and it filled all the house where they were sitting. And there appeared unto them cloven tongues like as of fire, and it sat upon each of them. And they were all filled with the Holy Ghost, and began to speak with other tongues, as the Spirit gave them utterance. (KJV).*

When Jesus was with the disciples, they witnessed extraordinary miracles through Him. They witnessed Him heal the sick and cast out demons, and when Jesus called them to follow Him, He ensured they were also equipped with the power to do these things. He gave them the power to crush the enemy and heal the people around them of their infirmities. Jesus taught them all He could and showed them what they were capable of. When He left, He did not leave them without that power. The Holy Spirit took His place on earth, making Him closer to them than He ever was. The same power that the disciples received is still available to you today. The same power that fell on them in that moment is in you today. You have the same power to cast out unclean spirits (powers) in your life and the lives of others. You have not been left to fend for yourself; you are not alone.

It is one thing to believe in the power of the Holy Spirit, but if you don't begin to believe that this power is actually living in you and begin to truly explore what that means for you, then it will be difficult to dominate your fears. Don't take my word for it. Get curious, explore the possibilities and seek confirmation for yourself.

The power of the Holy Spirit is available to everyone who is still alive on this earth, no matter their age, race, marital status or family background; it doesn't discriminate. If you are battling an addiction that has you afraid to dream big, this power can reside in you. If you did not believe in God even 10 seconds ago and you are now starting to find out more about who He is, the Holy Spirit can live in you if you decide to receive Him now. The power of the Holy Spirit is never truly lost, so if you accepted once but drifted at some point, you can reclaim it right now. All you have to do is just invite Him in. Just like with the air you breathe, you can take in as much as you need, as often as you need, whenever you need it, and it will never run out.

Worthy Of Power

The Holy Spirit doesn't only give life to our physical and spiritual bodies, He also gives life to our vision and purpose. When you connect with the Holy Spirit, you receive a true vision for the course of your life. There are a number of gifts that you may also receive and with these gifts you'll be able to complete the work that God created you to do and achieve the vision that you have been given. There are seven gifts (see 1 Corinthians 12), but ultimately, they all sum up to one gift and that is power from the Holy Spirit.

You are worthy of this power and the gifts that come with it. There is none who is perfect in this walk with Christ. Thankfully, we serve a God who looks beyond our faults and forgives our follies. Therefore, you don't need to listen to the enemy when he tries to convince you that you have gone too far and done too much to walk in your power.

Likewise, fear doesn't have to prevent you from doing what God is calling you to do.

The setbacks don't define you, and despite what you may have gone through and the level of fear in your life, you are entitled to claim your power.

Power Line

If you desire to see lasting changes in your family, then you'll need to get access to the power of the Holy Spirit. By accepting this power, your fears are not the only ones that will be dominated. We're not just talking about overcoming your addictions, establishing your own kingdom wealth, receiving higher education for yourself, or bringing back the happiness to your own marriage. When you accept the Holy Spirit, you are establishing a power line that will transcend all generations. Your children will not know what it means to allow fear to stop their progress; addiction won't hold them captive; their children will not be afraid to take the necessary steps to alleviate poverty; your offspring will gain the opportunity to obtain higher education and the things that plagued the marriages in your time will be no match for the power that you get access to. By making the decision to utilize your own power, you would have created a set of powerful ladies who can break generational curses, break the spirit of poverty and sickness, sever all other strongholds and demolish fear. Your bloodline will be filled with visionaries who understand that in their strength they are weak, but with the power of God, nothing can stop them.

If generational power is what you seek, then you have to get to that place of unwavering belief. The Holy Spirit is the source, and as a daughter of the King, that power is available to you and everyone else connected to you. When life throws us curveballs and we don't receive what we prayed for, it is hard to understand, let alone believe in this power.

There have been moments in my life when I got so discouraged and depressed I could barely even make it out of bed. In these moments of feeling utterly powerless, it became easy to sink into unbelief, questioning if God even cares, but as I reflect I can truly say that it is because of my firm belief in the presence of this power and the feeling that maybe something will work out that I was able to pull through. When you look to God, trust in His Spirit and His power then, His grace will keep you going when you cannot find the strength to go on. There is a line in a song by Kevin Downswell that says, *"When I come to the end of myself, Father carry me..."* Sis, that song has been my anthem throughout recent events and those words were often the only thing I could utter as a prayer to the Lord for Him to sustain me during difficult moments of fear, anxiety, and doubt.

In life, you may experience periods that can only be explained as reaching the end of who you have the capability to be and what you have the capacity to do on your own. This is when you'll need to keep your eyes fixed on God and trust that He will not leave you at the end but will provide His power for you to push beyond what you thought was going to be your final destination in life.

When things start to crumble, focus on God's ability to make a new path and His unconditional love for you, turn your attention to the power within, and try to remember that you are never alone, never without strength, and never forgotten. Don't lose hope; wherever dark place you may find yourself in because of fear, God will never leave you there. Remember that wherever you are and wherever you go, you carry a power that is able to make dead things live and renew the right frame of mind that can keep you going even beyond what you think you are capable of.

Do it for your power line!

Power Struggle

The closer we get to the Lord the harder, the devil will try to pull us away from Him. The more we try to develop the power that resides in us, the more the enemy will try to destroy it. For every action there is an equal and opposite reaction *(Newton's third Law)*. Where there is up, there is down; where there is "good air" there is "bad air,' and where there are the powers of God, there are also the powers of the enemy.

Carbon dioxide exists in our surroundings just the same as oxygen. This means we will not be able to prevent this "bad air" from entering our bodies. Carbon dioxide is also formed in our body during processes such as cellular respiration. So this bad air can enter our body directly from our environment and can also be developed through a series of activities that take place within us.

Therefore, even though we inhale about 0.4% carbon dioxide, we actually exhale approximately 4.4% of it. We cannot entirely prevent this "bad air" from getting in, but our body has a system that ensures that it goes out. This system also ensures that the good air that we need remains in us. Without this system our bodies would have too much "bad air," which would weaken the cells, resulting in us not having enough energy to survive. Without this internal filtration system, we would feel uncomfortable, weak and miserable as oxygen fights on its own to keep us alive.

Now if the Holy Spirit is the good air, then consider the powers of the devil as the bad air. Fear can directly enter our mind based on the things that we experience in life, and it can also be cultivated as a result of other elements within us such as unforgiveness, intrusive thoughts and depression. We will explore the role that these elements play in increasing fear in upcoming chapters.

The powers of God and the powers of the enemy will always be at odds with each other within and around us. There is always a struggle going on to decide which power can stay and which power can go; which power should die and which power should grow. In order to prevent the powers of the enemy from gaining control, it is important that you develop your own spiritual filtration systems. You need to do all you can to ensure that the powers of God remain dominant within and around you so that these powers can help with the execution of your vision and the overall quality of your life.

The power of the Holy Spirit can be separated into sub-powers and so too can the power of the enemy. In this book, we will take a look at the following forces as we try to develop a better understanding of how to effectively show up as the woman you have envisioned and create a system that will dominate the forces that are in direct opposition to your vision.

Sub-Powers of the Holy Spirit:

1. The Power of Prayer
2. The Power of Peace
3. The Power of Preparation
4. The Power of Faith

Opposing Powers

1. The Power of Fear
2. The Power of Unforgiveness
3. The Power of Depression

Already A Winner

The struggles that we face and the battle going on inside us can make it really difficult to effectively navigate our daily lives.

The internal struggles we experience can lead to mental health issues or illnesses and can also lead to suicide. With all that is happening within us, it is no wonder that showing up and executing our vision can be difficult. God has a plan and purpose for your life, and that is irrevocably the truth, but there are forces that aggressively challenge this purpose so it can be difficult to keep pursuing it. The power struggle can affect the way we show up at work, the way we think, how we relate to others, and the actions that we make. The level of fear that we experience can make stepping into our vision next to impossible.

When we get to the point where we believe that things are just too difficult for us to handle, that is when the devil presents the option to give up.

"Why bother?", he says. "Can't you see that there is no way you can make it? Don't you see that you are making a fool of yourself by trying to push on? Don't you see how weak and hopeless your efforts have been?"

Maybe he starts attacking your loved ones and you start to think, "What use is prayer when it can't stop sickness? My children are lost to me and there is nothing I can do to get them back on the right track. We will never be able to have enough money to provide for ourselves much less pursue vision."

Sis, believe this; no matter how hard these opposing powers might try, they are no match for the power of the Holy Spirit ,because this power is and will always be victorious. Understand that the powers that belong to God will always win. This, therefore, means that whatever you go through in life, you can never be defeated. The negative thoughts and invitation to give up can be dominated by the power of the Holy Spirit who is strong in you. When you allow the power of the Holy Spirit in you to fight against suicidal thoughts, anxiety, depression, insecurities, doubt, self-hate, disappointment, unforgiveness, fear, and all other sub-powers of the enemy, you'll be victorious.

God loves each and every one of us, and there is nothing that can separate us from this love that He has towards us (see Romans 8:38-39). So the devil can try all he wants, but even if he drags us to the darkest pit and floods our mind and body with fear and confusion, we will never be completely cut off from the power of the Holy Spirit, and with this power we will win every battle.

Without the power of the Holy Spirit, we will always be living our lives at 50% capacity or even less. Regardless of what is going on in and around you, your vision remains resolute. In order to execute this vision, you have to develop a system that constantly expels the powers of the enemy. With the power of the Holy Spirit living in you, you can do that and so much more.

Purposed for Power

Moreover, whom he did predestinate, them he also called: and whom he called, them he also justified: and whom he justified, them he also glorified.
Romans 8:30 – (KJV)

We can't talk about vision without addressing purpose. A vision is a clear mental image of what the future will or can look like as a result of wisely crafted plans. Purpose, on the other hand, speaks to the reason for which this vision was created. The two go hand in hand because in order for you to develop and execute your vision, you'll need to understand why you were created and why this vision was given to you. For example, a woman who knows that she was created to care for the sick may develop the vision of being a doctor and strive for this goal, while someone who has a passion for imparting knowledge may dream of being a teacher.

Your vision can also clarify your purpose. God might provide you with a glimpse of who you can be, which will confirm the reason for which He created you. Either way, having a clear concept of why you want to pursue a particular goal can provide the drive you need to move past your fears.

Life is multifaceted, so it would be safe to argue that purpose is not defined by a singular place or moment but rather a cluster of kingdom assignments that may eventually lead to a major mission that you were predestined to complete. This means that purpose can be found in every moment.

As you consider purpose and what it means to show up as your highest self, you should try to shed the mindset that you have to wait until you get to a specific place in life to be the woman you envision. Sometimes we think "When God blesses me with this specific thing, then I will start to be who I want to be and do the things I want to do." Of course, certain things that you desire might require specific resources that you genuinely need to wait for, but you can still try to find a few things that you can start to do right now. You can start showing up as your highest self without having everything perfectly figured out. Start making small changes to the way you do things in your current situation. It might feel odd at first, and you might think you are wasting your time, but the small steps will eventually add up to noticeable changes as you seek to improve yourself every day and move towards your vision. Do you see why the enemy chooses to find ways to attack, distract and discourage you every day and in everything you do? If you give up or slack off in one area of your life, chances are, giving up and making excuses will become a trend that eventually leads to you living a life where you are fearful of trying anything new. By doing this, you will miss the chance to execute your kingdom assignments.

The position you are currently in at work, school, in your family, or at church might not be ideal, but once you are aligned with the Spirit of God and trust that He is the one who led you to where you currently are, then you have reached an important aspect of your journey towards realising your main vision. Likewise, sometimes our fears come from the overwhelming feelings we get when we think about the big picture (the overall vision). Breaking things down and doing smaller activities related to the big picture may improve your confidence in your ability to handle the responsibilities associated with your main vision.

God is intentional; He does nothing by accident. There are lessons to be learned, people to impact, or opportunities to capitalize on in this moment of your life. You might be struggling and feel like giving up but keep pushing. Purpose encompasses your entire journey through life and is comprised of experiences that will help to shape you into the woman that God wants you to be; the woman who will be able to carry out the plans He has already mapped out.

It is quite fine to desire more than what you are currently experiencing. In fact, it is by God's design that you are currently craving a life more impactful and fulfilling. You were not made to stay at one stage of your life forever. You were made to grow; constantly changing and evolving into a better version of yourself. There is power connected to your vision and to your journey on this earth. Just as you were created to fulfill your purpose, it was also intended for you to receive and carry the power that will be required to achieve it. It is this power that will propel you to the next level of your life for you to pursue the next level of your purpose.

Earlier we talked about purpose being a series of assignments that can be found in each stage of life. Well, as you progress to each level, the magnitude of your fear will grow to match the level of your assignment. Fear will have you questioning your abilities, and it will try to force you to give up on everything you might be working to attain. The devil will have you believe that dominating your fear and moving on to the next stage is impossible, but God assures us that not only is it possible, it has been predestined.

If you are one of those women who believe you are ordinary, then allow me to lovingly challenge this misconception. Our extraordinary Father doesn't create ordinary people. You might see yourself as insignificant, unworthy of chasing the dreams that you have for yourself, but this is what you were born to do.

You have to consider that you might be having trouble showing up as the woman you've envisioned because you are finding it difficult to believe that you can actually be her. In other words, though you can picture yourself doing the things that you want to, there might be a sense of disassociation because these things just don't match up to the way you see yourself in your current state.

Your progress will be hindered until you start to believe that you are more than your fears, past mistakes, and failures. The goal is to actually carry out your vision and fulfill your purpose, but you won't be able to even start the process until you start believing that you are more than who the enemy has tried to convince you that you are. You are far more than the labels that society places on you.

You are holy and beloved (see Colossians 3:12); you are an heir of God (see Romans 8:17); and you are special, precious in God's eyes (see Isaiah 43:4). When you start to feel unqualified, unworthy and incapable of carrying out your goals, you might even question whether it really is the enemy attacking your God-given image or if this is really just who you are. You might start to think, "Maybe I really am all those things; maybe I'm just fooling myself into thinking that I can start this business or this non-profit organization; or maybe I really am too old or too young to do this." These negative thoughts are not true and have been created to cause doubt and feed insecurities. If you feel the need to create change in a specific area of your surroundings or become a better version of yourself, then you should go for it!

You have the power to make your dreams a reality. You can push past thoughts of inferiority and step into the vision that has been laid on your heart. It is not a coincidence that these ideas have been in your mind for as long as you can remember. You were made to surpass your expectations and those of others and create things that can move the world. You were born to receive the power that you'll need to make these things happen.

Be More, Do More

Your identity is not defined by what you do on this earth but rather by who you are in Christ. Likewise, you are not your purpose; instead, your purpose is an extension of who you are. You cannot remove Christ from your journey to execute your vision, and striving to become more like Him will assist you in dominating your fears and executing this vision.

According to John 14:12-14, we were destined to receive the power that will enable us to do far more than what Jesus did when He was on earth. These things were world-changing miracles that saved lives and caused people to change their lives in order to live as God required. If you were made to do even more than this, it is safe to say that you were made to release even more power as well. This means the enemy will increase the level of fear. Developing a spiritual filtration system means that you will constantly be improving as a woman of God. Hence, as you become more like the woman that God created you to be, you will gradually begin to develop the power to do more of what He has created you to do. That being said, your fears will begin to look quite small in the grand scheme of things.

On your way to executing your vision, you need to consider the characteristics that made it possible for Jesus to bypass His own fears, and fulfill His own purpose. Yes, even Jesus faced fear and anxiety on His journey (see Luke 22:44), but in those moments, He was able to obtain power and strength from God and remain confident about who He is. You have access to even more of that power through the Holy Spirit, so it is within your capability to conquer any level of fear that you are currently experiencing and accomplish that big dream you have been given.

In discussions about purpose, you really can't speak too much about love and compassion because, as you know, love triumphs over evil. We also know that fear is a weapon of evil, so it only makes sense to include love as one of the ways to dominate fear as you strive to execute your vision, and since our multifaceted Father is love, then the ultimate way to gain and release an unlimited supply of Love is to keep close to Him as much as possible. On His way to accomplishing His mission, Jesus did all He could for others at each step of His journey. His characteristics are what fuelled His drive and kept Him going, and one of the major characteristics that He possessed was love.

Even though He is the Son of God and carried around a power that was far greater than anyone around Him could even imagine, He remained humble and showed compassion, love, patience, and kindness. By doing this, not only was He able to make it to His destination, but He was able to impact the lives of many others during His time on earth by showing them that they too could obtain and unleash that same power, and this is still possible today.

As you strive to pursue your destiny, try to focus on developing your confidence in Christ and being more like Him. I know we're talking about fulfilling your purpose, implementing your vision, and showing up as your best self but doing more also includes helping people to come to terms with their own ability to receive power and demolish their fears. If you know that you were called to be a leader but your current assignment requires you to follow someone and help them to accomplish their purpose, then do so with humility. The more you focus on being like Christ, the more you'll be able to accomplish.

Your highest self will be a reflection of the level that you are in Christ. The higher you are in Christ, and the more you strive to be like Him, the more you'll be able to accomplish.

In order to be elevated in your life, you have to adopt the characteristics of Christ. Keeping your knowledge and skills locked away out of fear that someone will steal your thunder and progress further than you will not get you to the height that you seek. In fact, the residual jealousy and self-righteousness will only drag you lower.

The field you want to enter is not too saturated, so there is no need to be intimidated or afraid of being overlooked. Just because you were destined for great things doesn't mean that others were not; there is enough power to go around. God has purposely left a spot open just for you because you were the one He created to fill it. However, if you don't allow Him to transform your heart by aligning yours with His, then you just might lose that spot to someone who has because His plans for you are mainly about building His Kingdom not about helping you to flex your successes. God's power and His heart go hand in hand, so even though you were made to receive His power, you cannot have it without first receiving His heart.

The power you possess is not for you to selfishly climb to the top of your field and worship yourself. Worship must always be directed towards God, and His power must always be used to impact the lives of others. So while others might be chasing the fame and glory that comes with doing more, as a woman filled with the power of the Holy Spirit, you should always remember to focus your attention on being more. On your way to achieving your goals, strive to be more compassionate, patient, humble, wise, selfless, and loving than even Jesus was. I mean, we will never be able to match His level, but it's a really good standard to live by. These characteristics will build your confidence, keep you connected to God and make it possible for you to push past your fears as you progress.

Going Beyond What Is Familiar

God has given us the ability and permission to try and achieve as much as we dare to chase after in all areas of our lives. Once you make the decision to progress, your abilities and power will increase along the way, and before you know it, you'll be living a life of abundance. Have you ever thought, "Wow! I did not know that I was capable of doing or creating that?" If you have, then get this, that was just a small drop in the bucket compared to what God has in store for you, but if you have not, then I encourage you to venture a bit further beyond what you have grown accustomed to. There is only so much that can astonish you in the Land of Familiar.

Now when you decide to take a step outside the box and get exposed to places and projects *[things attached to your vision]* that you have never encountered before, you might get a bit intimidated, and you might start to feel as if you don't belong there; you might begin to feel like an imposter. That is just a part of the process as the new you adjust to the change. The longer you remain in the new spaces, the more you'll begin to learn the requirements needed for success, and the easier things will eventually become. Don't run back to the old places because you feel out of place in the new ones.

Having a routine is good, but if you are not willing to switch things up now and then, that routine may leave you stuck and hinder your ability to execute your vision. In order to get more done and progress, you have to be constantly moving and seeking experiences beyond what you are normally comfortable with.

The fear of change can sometimes prevent us from pursuing our vision. Sometimes we know exactly what to do, but our fears keep us stuck in a loop of monotony and complacency, never exploring what is beyond our comfort zone. We may experience a fear of what lies beyond, a fear of having to return after failing to accomplish what we set out to, and a fear of realizing on our way that we were never special in the first place, just ordinary all along. These fears are often amplified when we tell someone about our vision, and they start to remind us about who we are and what we're known for.

"What do you mean you want more out of life? This is all you get. You could never do these things; don't you remember what happened last time you tried?"

God's power, purpose, and vision go hand in hand, and you were born with the capacity to receive that power, discover your purpose, dominate your fears, and execute your vision. The negative opinions of others should not keep you from saying yes to God and venturing outside your comfort zone.

The more you show up, the more fear will show up also. When fear tries to get you to quit or return to what you are familiar with instead of moving towards your destiny, rely on God's ability to lead you and keep going towards your dream. The truth is, we really cannot completely get rid of fear while on earth, but your unwavering decision to do things a bit differently and continue in spite of the unknown will definitely make it easier for you as time goes by. So, Miss Visionary, dare to go beyond your comfort zone and keep going because if more is what you desire, there will always be a way to obtain it. There is nothing wrong with pausing when fear comes up; there is no rule that says you cannot take a break when you get overwhelmed. However, when you pause, don't just look for ways to distract you from the fear. Instead, find rest and peace in God as you ask Him to guide you through fearful circumstances.

If you feel like there is something inside you that needs to be birthed, then keep pursuing it. Spend time with God, ask Him to help you develop the right plan, connect you with the right people and provide the right resources. Keep reading the Word, keep thinking about your dream, keep that spark alive. If you are hungry for something beyond what you are currently experiencing and you know in your heart that there is something out there with your name on it, even if you are not quite sure what it is, just keep seeking clarity. If the things that normally make you content no longer feel like enough, or the place you thought would make you happy is not what you expected, then you can make the decision to start moving towards your next assignment.

Don't allow fear to kill your dream and keep you trapped in the zones of familiar. Keep hoping and keep believing. Maybe you are at a stage in your life where you just know in your heart that this just cannot be it for you. You might be trying to conform, trying to operate in your normal routine, and trying to show up the way everyone else around you is showing up, the way you are used to showing up, but in your heart, you keep thinking that it is just not for you anymore. You cannot quite put your finger on it, but this great sense of endless possibility just came out of nowhere, and now you cannot sit still. You cannot go back to living the way you used to; you keep trying to but that feeling deep inside just keeps hinting that there is so much more that you can achieve.

This desire for more will never go away because that is how life is supposed to be. You have been purposed for power, and the dream that you can't seem to get out of your head is what you were born to do.

The Power Of You

There might be moments when you think, "Why did God give me, of all people, this specific vision? Yvette is a way better person than I am. She would be the best one to do it." The vision you have been given is good, the work you must do to execute this vision is good, and you are the best person to do it. Even if your fear of failure doesn't subside, you should still pursue your dreams because since God is the one who started this thing in you, He will stick with you until it has been completed (see Philippians 1:6).

Your unique vision is specific to a unique need that exists in the world, and you have been charged to execute this vision because you are the person who can make an impact. Yvette has her set of skills that make her powerful, and you have yours.

Once you are able to visualize what you want your life to look like, you are the one who will have to get up and make it happen. The Lord will empower you to make your dream a reality, but after that, if you do nothing, God does nothing. If you want to see what it is like to live as the woman you have envisioned, then you are the one who will have to take the first step so that His plans can be set into motion. The power that you possess is limited only by the extent to which you use it. If you rely on it to get you to a job that you might not even like anymore, it will get you there, and if you set out to discover what lies beyond that job, then it will get you there too, but this can only happen if you choose to start doing the things that it will take to propel you further.

When it comes to the vision you have been given, it is not a mistake. You are worthy of the things you seek; you can become the woman you want to be in Christ; you do have the power to become the woman you want to be, and you can dominate your fears. The enemy doesn't have any power over you. The powers that he utilizes to keep you down are no match for the power of God that you have the ability to wield. The enemy might fill your head with fear and doubt, but you have been given the power to fight back (see Genesis 3:15). The power that resides in you is far greater than any other power that might be against you. It is in you! The power that you are seeking is already within you. You were predestined to do greater works, and the only one who can stop you from doing this work is you.

This power has been given to you on purpose, and you need to start believing that. It doesn't matter what has been said about you, God has set you apart, He still cares for you, and He still wants you to make your vision a reality. He still wants to use you to bring others to Him, and He still wants to get you to that elevated place of abundance in Him.

Do you know why the Bible refers to the church as a woman? Because it is precious to God. It is protected even when persecuted, valuable even when the world looks down on it, and necessary for the salvation of souls. That is you! That is how God sees you! The enemy might try to frustrate you, condemn you, and use fear to drive you out of your calling, but you are the church. That means once you remain close to God and receive the power that has been offered to you, there is nothing the devil can do to stop the works that God wants to do through you. This power-walk is a partnership between you and the Holy Spirit. You have a role to play in the way you show up, and you have a role to play as it relates to the level of power that can show up in you.

It has been given to you, but you have to decide whether or not you want to use it. When you feel the urge to head out and move forward, the decision to make the first move will be entirely up to you. Sure, you don't know where the steps will lead, but God already does, and you can trust that He will never lead you somewhere and leave you there. He will be there every step of the way.

Pretending that you don't feel the urge to do more will not help you in the long run. I know you have bills to pay, and sometimes you might think, "Why doesn't God just make things happen then; doesn't He see that I have a mortgage and responsibilities? I don't have time to just pick up and pursue this dream; there are people counting on me." Maybe you really want to do this thing, but you just cannot seem to find the time. You can trust that God knew all the responsibilities that you would have before giving you the vision, and once you make the decision to move, He will make provisions to take care of everything that you might be worried about. You and your family will not starve while you pursue this vision. Even though we all wish a couple more hours could be added to the clock so we can do the things we want, you have to make sacrifices in order to achieve your goals. Your plate might be heavy, but if you want to experience that kingdom overflow, then you have to make room for God.

That little push you might be getting to take some time and write that book, start that business or go back to school is intentional, and you know in your heart that you won't be able to live comfortably until you do it. There are people out there waiting on you, people who are looking for the kind of expertise you can provide. Believe in the power of you. You are capable of so much more than what you are doing now, and even if you get to that Michelle Obama level and still want to get more out of life, you can. Nothing on this earth can stop you.

The Lord doesn't start something unless He intends to finish it. If you have visualized the life that you desire, then He will help you to get it, and no amount of fear can stop that once you make up your mind to pursue it. You are enough, you are worthy, and you are capable of making things work.

Things will always come up. There will always be something to do; some reason why you should not go after what you want. However, you owe it to yourself to maximize your potential and use the power that was purposefully given to you. You owe it to yourself to try.

The Power of God

"And Moses said unto God, Behold, when I come unto the children of Israel, and shall say unto them, The God of your fathers hath sent me unto you; and they shall say to me, What is his name? what shall I say unto them? And God said unto Moses, I Am That I Am: and he said, Thus shalt thou say unto the children of Israel, I Am hath sent me unto you. And God said moreover unto Moses, Thus shalt thou say unto the children of Israel, the Lord God of your fathers, the God of Abraham, the God of Isaac, and the God of Jacob, hath sent me unto you: this is my name for ever, and this is my memorial unto all generations. Go, and gather the elders of Israel together, and say unto them, The Lord God of your fathers, the God of Abraham, of Isaac, and of Jacob, appeared unto me, saying, I have surely visited you, and seen that which is done to you in Egypt: And I have said, I will bring you up out of the affliction of Egypt unto the land of the Canaanites, and the Hittites, and the Amorites, and the Perizzites, and the Hivites, and the Jebusites, unto a land flowing with milk and honey."
Exodus 3:13–17 (KJV)

"**God a God'"** *(God is God)* is a term used by Jamaicans during times of difficulties and uncertainties. Essentially, it means that since God is who He is, He knows what He is doing, He will be able to fix any issue in our lives, and He will be able to deliver us from problematic circumstances. When uttered, this means that we trust that God will see things through.

You may be feeling as if you are in a strange season in your life, as do most of us. Not only do we have to deal with the aftermath of a global pandemic, but there are economic challenges due to a war between two countries. These things might have you thinking, "How am I going to pursue this vision in the middle of all this? Why would God now require me to be heading out when it seems as if we should be staying in and storing things up in this time of chaos? I mean, I did start making plans to pursue my dreams, but things are changing now. Everything is increasing; oil prices, gas, food, even two of the most precious things on this earth that gives so much joy; our beloved bread and delicious Jamaican patty are becoming too much to afford. Now God is asking me to spend money on classes and business plans, recording studios and books? How will the promises that He made still come to pass? How can I still receive those promises? How can I still execute my plans? Doesn't He see what's going on in the world!?"

This might look like a season of chaos and increased prices, but to God it is a season of waiting, trusting, having faith in Him, maintaining your loyalty to Him, and an increase in your status as a lady with power.

The Promise

The Israelites were in captivity, facing hardship and living under extremely difficult circumstances. God saw what was happening to them and decided that He wanted to deliver them and elevate their status in the world. They were about to move from slave to sacred. Because He wanted to give them more than what they were experiencing at the time, He called Moses and sent him to lead them out of their hardship. While they were still in Egypt going through hard times, He promised to take them to a place where they had never been before, where they would be able to become more than they were at the time. While they were still being persecuted, He promised freedom and redemption, a place of peace where they could flourish and live out the rest of their days as they pleased. When they were convinced that these were all God's promises and that they would be able to receive these promises, the Israelites gathered their belongings and proceeded toward this promised land.

While they were traveling, they ended up in harsh environments. God promised to take them to this wonderful place, but they were always finding themselves in the desert with their enemies chasing after them. They were often without food and water, which made them question why God brought them out into the desert to die. They complained saying: *"...because there were no graves in Egypt, hast thou taken us away to die in the wilderness? wherefore hast thou dealt thus with us, to carry us forth out of Egypt? Is not this the word that we did tell thee in Egypt, saying, let's alone, that we may serve the Egyptians? For it had been better for us to serve the Egyptians, than that we should die in the wilderness" (Exodus 14:11-12 - KJV).* They were afraid of being killed by their enemies, afraid of starvation, and afraid of not making it to the Promised Land, so they grumbled and complained whenever they encountered unexpected peril.

Hold Your Peace

"And Moses said unto the people, Fear ye not, stand still, and see the salvation of the Lord, which he will shew to you today: for the Egyptians whom ye have seen today, ye shall see them again no more

forever. The Lord shall fight for you, and ye shall hold your peace."
(Exodus 14:13-14 - KJV).

On your way to becoming the woman in your vision, the enemy will use fear to intimidate you. He will try to frustrate, confuse and discourage you so that you'll think you are alone on your faith walk. Fear, your circumstances, and the people who might be out to dampen your spirit are no match for the God who is leading you each step of the way. The Lord released His mighty power on the Egyptians who were after His people, and cleared a path for them to make it through the obstacles they were facing. Rest assured that He will use His power to do the same for you. Don't dwell on the places you left behind just because of the disorder that might be ensuing around you now. The God you serve will make a path for you and take you through the chaos. The road to your vision will not be without trials and setbacks, but you'll get there as long as you rely on God to bring you through uncertainties.

Hold your peace and stand your ground against the attacks of the enemy, and pay no attention to what may be after your vision. Keep looking ahead; a way will be made for you to continue on your journey. Every roadblock will be cleared, every "no" will turn into a "yes," and you'll be introduced to every person who is connected to the completion of your assignment.

Stand firm in your faith and pursue your marriage, children, business, book and everything else that may be associated with your Promised Land. Stand firm for that house you are planning to get, the degree that you are after, and the promotion God says He is going to give you. Whatever God promised you is still possible. When fear tries to convince you to go back to the place where you were unmotivated, persecuted, and unproductive, don't turn back. God moved you from a place where your creativity was being stifled, and your opinions were not being heard, and He promised you your own space where you would be free to do what you like. Some people might not like that. They like to see you totally dependent on them. They want you around to help them with their own dreams, so they will do anything in their power to get you to give up on yours. Stand your ground because God is with you, and when you cannot fight for yourself, He will fight for you. He knows you cannot handle everything on your own. He knows your strengths and weaknesses, and He is more than capable of fighting the battles you cannot fight yourself.

The Lord will place Himself between you and everything that tries to break you. He made a promise to you, and He will fulfill that promise no matter what.

Be still and watch your words. Be careful what you say or do in this season of your life, lest you miss out on the promises of God. If you make it past this, you'll receive all that you ever asked for and even more. If you continue to navigate your season of uncertainty without complaining and remain faithful to God, He is going to blow your mind. Your perspective regarding the situation you are in may cause you to make a decision that can cost you your vision. If you focus on chaos, then that is all you'll see, but if you focus on God, you'll be able to see the clear path He has laid out you.

You Will Not Starve

"And the children of Israel said unto them, would to God we had died by the hand of the Lord in the land of Egypt, when we sat by the flesh pots, and when we did eat bread to the full; for ye have brought us forth into this wilderness, to kill this whole assembly with hunger." (Exodus 16: 3 - KJV).

Those were the words spoken by the Israelites as they travelled towards God's promise. There may have been moments when your cupboards have been dry. You have probably left your 9-5 after being told by God that He has a better place for you, only to end up being unable to provide for yourself and your family. At this moment, you might start to think, "I was getting a great salary where I was before. Even though I hated what I did and was constantly overlooked and put down, at least at the end of the month there was a sure way for me to pay my bills."

I am not going to tell you that the bills will not pile up; this is not the point where I tell you that if you follow your dream, your cup will overflow daily. What I can tell you is that God will never allow it to be empty for long, and if you put your trust in Him, you and your family will not starve. I can tell you that if you keep moving forward and don't allow the darkness to let you stray from God's principles and instructions, then He will provide a feast in every area of your life.

There may be moments where you run out of resources, but that will only make room for the overflow that God will eventually provide. He is that powerful; that is what He does. He sees your needs, and He provides. Even if you end up sitting in the dark with only dust in your cupboard, keep going; don't give up. That's just how it has to be for a while. When you make a big switch in your lifestyle, it is going to take time to get back on your feet again. You may not continue to get the big feast that you are used to, but God did not tell you to leave where you were just to leave you hanging. He provided manna for the Israelites, and it was just enough to get them by on their journey. It was just enough to keep them strong and sustain them while they were on their way to the glorious land of prosperity and abundance that the Lord had promised.

He will sustain you and your family on your way to your version of overflow.

Seek God For Yourself

The Israelites had Moses delivering God's messages to them, but you have direct access to God; you can speak to Him directly and receive His directions for your life. They verbalized their concerns, but it was in the form of grumbling and complaining. Whenever they faced challenges, instead of asking God to help them, they brought their negativity to Moses.

Building your own relationship will give you far more insight into God's power and far more clarity about the details of your vision than if you were to receive information from someone else. Connecting with Him will reduce the fear, anxiety, and confusion that come with moving toward something you are not familiar with. He already knows your situation, so instead of speaking poorly about it to others, bring your concerns to God yourself. It is good to seek the opinions of others, but you'll be able to feel more confident about God's ability to lead you towards your vision when you take the time to hear from Him yourself.

Power Is In The Dry Seasons

"And it came to pass, when Pharaoh had let the people go, that God led them not through the way of the land of the Philistines, although that was near; for God said, Lest peradventure the people repent when they see war, and they return to Egypt: But God led the people about, through the way of the wilderness of the Red sea: and the children of Israel went up harnessed out of the land of Egypt. And Moses took the bones of Joseph with him: for he had straitly sworn the children of Israel, saying, God will surely visit you; and ye shall carry up my bones away hence with you. And they took their journey from Succoth, and encamped in Etham, in the edge of the wilderness." (Exodus 13:17-20 – KJV).

It is okay to embrace dry places. You were brought there deliberately, and even though it is uncomfortable and unfamiliar, you are going the right way. Coincidences don't occur when you are following Christ. If you find yourself in a place that doesn't look as resplendent as the one you see in your vision, try not to worry about it. God is still there with you; His power is still mighty in dry places.

Wherever you are in your life, you are there for a reason, and I want to encourage you to embrace it. God did not lead you into the dry place to leave you there. His words are true, and His promises are yes and amen, even in the dry places. If you trust God to lead you through this place, you'll be able to handle anything that comes up against you after. The lessons you'll learn and the people you'll meet are crucial for your next position in life.

There is deliverance and protection in this dry place, and you can still have access to peace and provision there. God's grace, favour, love, and joy are still in this dry place. Don't think that the things God has already given you or promised to give you will vanish when you face troubles and trials. He is still present in these seasons. The financial breakthrough or whatever it is you may be believing God for in this season of your life can still be yours; just allow Him to guide you and trust in His timing. His power will sustain you in your dry seasons. He is with you even when you cannot really feel His presence or understand why He took you the long way around. He knows what He is doing. Don't be perplexed by the dry place on your way to receiving your blessings.

Confirm Your Path

You need to ensure that the path you are on is the one God has prepared for you. That vision you are chasing needs to be from God. You don't want to waste time and energy, not to mention money and resources, just to end up somewhere that you were not supposed to be in the first place. You also cannot allow your fear of going through the dry places to take you on a path that was not meant for you because it seems easier. Many are the plans in our course, but it is the Lord's plans and purpose that we should follow. Those are the only plans that will get you to the place that you have envisioned.

Stop knocking on doors in places you were not even supposed to be. That emptiness you may be feeling after getting to the places you worked so hard to get to is possibly because you were never meant to be there in the first place. You cannot strive to get to a high place without even allowing God to show you where that is supposed to be. Give up your need for control so God can steer you in the right direction. To do this, you have to be willing to humble yourself and be patient as He gives you the answer. You have to be willing to completely give up the plans you have because they might not line up with the ones He has in mind for you. Relinquishing control can do wonders to alleviate the fears that we have regarding the path we must take.

No matter how hard this might be, keep an open mind and heart because it will be so worth it when you finally see what you'll be getting instead. There is absolutely nothing wrong with being ambitious and wanting more for yourself, but this also has to be what God wants for you because anything else would be pointless.

So that project or opportunity that you thought was best for you but it did not come through and now you are thinking, "What am I going to do and, God, how could You allow this to happen?" God did not tell you He was going to do that; you told that to yourself. One of the wonderful things about God is that He has no problem helping us to bounce back, so even if we follow our own path and end up somewhere we should not have beeb, God can put us back on track once we ask.

The purpose and vision that God has for you are not common; they consist of Kingdom promises that will take you to Kingdom territories. Those are the territories that the enemy uses fear to keep you from. Ensure that the territories you are pursuing are those that God has appointed for you; ensure that you pray and commit your vision to God. If you pursue something that was not ordained by God, you may end up being confused and inefficient in your tasks. The Lord will make your path straight only if you lay down the plans you have for yourself and get in alignment with the plans He has for you.

Don't Settle For Counterfeit

"And Moses and Aaron went in unto Pharaoh, and they did so as the Lord had commanded: and Aaron cast down his rod before Pharaoh, and before his servants, and it became a serpent. Then Pharaoh also called the wise men and the sorcerers: now the magicians of Egypt, they also did in like manner with their enchantments. For they cast down every man his rod, and they became serpents: but Aaron's rod swallowed up their rods." (Exodus 7:10-12 - KJV).

If you want a reminder of how powerful God is, just take a look at the story of Moses and Pharaoh in the book of Exodus. God really did some amazing things to show what He is capable of. If you want to see what He can do in your life, then all you have to do is ask.

When Pharaoh witnessed these extraordinary acts of God, he wanted some form of explanation. So he called his wise men and sorcerers, and they were able to do the same things. God turned a staff into a snake, and Pharaoh's sorcerers turned their staffs into snakes as well. Pharaoh thought that because the snakes looked the same they were all the same, produced by the same power.

In the end, God's power, which is superior, devours anything that the enemy tries to replicate. That was evident when all the other snakes were consumed by the one that was created through God's power. You'll also encounter powers, signs, and wonders that appear in the form of godliness. You'll be introduced to people and taken to places that seem to have been provided by God. As you strive to abide in God and depend on His power, you'll come across things that appear similar to the original promises and vision that it will be almost impossible to decipher which is genuine. At this point, you'll need to put these "knockoffs" to the test (see 1 John 4:1). Test the forces that you come in contact with before making decisions related to your vision. You don't have to make any commitments prematurely; the true power will be revealed through patience.

Don't settle for counterfeit; you are going to need the real thing in order to execute your vision and gain true fulfillment. True power comes from God, and only that power can dominate fear, insecurities, depression, and confusion.

You may also experience moments of uncertainty and weariness, which might tempt you to choose the things that seem easier or more readily accessible. If you are waiting for a husband, a financial breakthrough, a child, an advancement in your career, or anything else that you need in order for you to be the woman in your vision, be patient. In other words, if something that resembles what you want shows up, don't allow impatience and weariness to cause you to settle for less than what you deserve. You need to turn your back on what looks like it could work, and keep your eyes on the real prize that God showed you because it will be a lot more rewarding. You don't want to be standing too close to the things trying to imitate the power of God when He gets ready to remove them. Those things will only drag you down with them.

When Pharaoh saw the things that God was able to do, he sent for persons who he thought were wise enough to provide him with a plausible explanation. Be careful who you take advice from as you move towards the execution of your vision. Be mindful of the things you listen to from people who might not believe in the power that God possesses and the things He can do for you. If you see God's hands in your life and you try to tell someone about the wonderful things that He is doing for you but they don't want to believe it, that is just fine. It's better to keep certain things to yourself anyway.

Don't allow people to lead you astray in this season of your life because you know the God you serve and the things He is capable of. Don't let them convince you to choose what seems 'rational' and 'conceivable.' The power that God possesses can do things that are beyond your wildest imagination.

Don't settle for the things you know are not associated with the power of God. Wait on God's promises; He will not withhold anything from you if you remain loyal to Him (see Psalm 84:11). You may think He is taking too long to provide the things you have asked for. It is a natural thing to want to go with what you can already see, but don't settle for counterfeit in this season of your life.

Likewise, you need to assess your circumstances, tear down ever ungodly altar, remove any idol that may have been established and ask God for discernment to see through the lies of every false doctrine. This is the time for you to be real with yourself. If you are serious about becoming that woman in your vision, you'll need to expose any false powers that might be at work in your life. The power of God cannot devour what you don't denounce and His power cannot work in your life, if you continue to operate under the power of idolatry. Prosperity in Christ is the only form that will truly add value to your life on earth and prepare you to live eternally. When you are confident that you are in alignment with the right power, then you'll be less fearful of what it will produce, and more confident in your chances of success.

The Israelites decided to set up their own god because of impatience and disobedience. After all the promises God made and all the times He provided for them, they still tried to replace Him.

When God's representative, Moses, departed from them, they could no longer see him, so they thought he was dead. Their only connection to God disappeared and instead of trusting that he would return and believing that God was still with them, they created their own god. They placed their trust in that god's ability to make them feel good. They created a golden calf and decided that since they could no longer hear from the God who led them out of Egypt, they would fashion something that would hopefully sustain them in their present environments.

Do you have a golden calf in your life? Have you been thinking that since you cannot feel God's presence, that means He is no longer with you? Have you sought comfort in your phone, Netflix, other people, your job or an addiction in hopes that these things will help you through difficult times?

The power of God is present even when you cannot sense it. He was still alive working things out for the Israelites back then, and He is still alive working things out for you now. Don't allow anything to take up the space that God needs to occupy in your life. Also, don't waste time that should be spent building your relationship with God on things that can be easily destroyed by Him. He revealed who He was to Moses so many years ago and He is still the same today. He is still present, still powerful and is still working to get you to your promised land.

There is nothing wrong with using your device and watching your favourite shows on Netflix. The Lord encourages rest and doesn't condemn leisurely activities. Just ensure that these things don't take up too much of your time and distract you from increasing the power inside of you. Remember, if the enemy cannot destroy your vision, he will find ways to distract you from pursing it.

The power that God possesses can get you through any fearful situation. By confirming your path, being obedient to His instructions and remaining loyal to Him, you won't be consumed by the fear that threatens to devour you. When you connect with God's power, it can do as much around you as it can within you.

The Power of Peace

Peace I leave with you, my peace I give unto you: not as the world giveth, give I unto you. Let not your heart be troubled, neither let it be afraid.
John 14:27 (KJV)

When we constantly look to our distress and focus on inadequacies, our mind will remain unsettled. When this happens we will not be able to clearly receive the instructions needed to move towards our next assignment.

In Judges 6, we're told about the Israelites who have once again found themselves in a sticky situation as a result of disobedience and idolatry. This time, the Lord chooses a Gideon to deliver the Israelites from the hands of their enemies, the Midianites. When the Lord said to Gideon, "Go in this might [strength] of yours, and you shall save Israel from the hand of the Midianites. Have I not sent you?" *(Judges 6:14 - KJV),* he was not convinced that he was the right guy for the job. He questioned his ability to save Israel by explaining that out of all the clans, his was the weakest and he was the weakest in his family. After listening to Gideon's concerns, God promised him that because He would be with him, when he was ready to strike, not a single Midianite would be left alive and the land would once again belong to them.

Gideon was still not convinced and asked God to show him a sign, and He obliged by enlisting the help of an angel. After seeing what the angel was able to do, Gideon was startled, but the Lord said to him, "Peace be unto thee; fear not: thou shalt not die." (Judges 6:23 - KVJ). After calming down, Gideon was able to receive the instructions needed to do what the Lord requested.

In the middle of his distress, the Lord provided Gideon with reassurance and peace before sending him on the mission that he was intended to accomplish. God is so deliberate and so patient with His people. He welcomes our concerns and has no problem providing answers when we humbly ask for His confirmation. Before God even told Gideon what to do, He ensured that he was in the right frame of mind to receive the instructions that He wanted to deliver. Gideon made his concerns known to the Lord so he could receive proof that this was his assignment and he was in fact the right person to complete it.

As you begin to consider the idea of becoming more than you are now and doing more than you thought you were capable of doing, you must utilize the power of peace. Your vision probably terrifies you because it is so far off from what you are used to. It is okay to release all the concerns and fears from your mind by speaking directly to God. Don't be afraid to question God about the things that you see yourself doing; who better to give you clarity than the one who gave you the vision? It is also okay if you are not quite sure if you are the right woman to do what you have visualized, and it is okay if you are not quite sure how to become the woman you have envisioned. Let the peace of God flood your mind so you can receive clarity. When fear steps up, then seek the Lord's peace. Share your worries with God and let Him know how you feel about the assignment you have been given. Tell Him your concerns; He welcomes them (see Philippians 4:6-7).

Allowing our fears to move from our minds to our mouths and to God's ears will make space for His peace which will reveal what we need in order to prevail.

Peace Reveals Strength

When God told Gideon that he was the one chosen to save the Israelites from the Midianites, the first thing he did was start to explain who he was. He started to remind God that he was from the weakest clan and that he was also the weakest in his family. What Gideon was actually doing was revealing his fears of failing in light of his perceived insecurities and shortcomings.

Sometimes we see things happening in our family, church, or community, and we pray to God for a way to change things, but when He reveals that we're the one He wants to use to do it, the magnitude of this plan seems so intimidating and so grand that we start to think He made a mistake by choosing us. We think or say thinks like: "I mean, come on, Lord, I'm a woman. How can I possibly do that? You think a high school dropout like me can do the things that You have shown me? I'm a teen mom, recovering drug addict, and a project of the ghetto; I can't do this." The fear of not being enough can stop us from even trying to see things from God's point of view. Admitting that we have these insecurities is a step in the right direction.

I know that there is life and death in the power of the tongue and that we should speak positively over our lives, but false positivity will only increase your fears. You have to reveal your fears so God can show you your strength.

Let's say you feel as though you are the weakest in your family, your job, your community, or church, in some aspects. Maybe you did not have a chance to make it to the level of education that your siblings did. Maybe you are still in a job that barely provides enough to pay your bills, and you keep getting overlooked for promotions, or maybe your family is not the most influential. You might be at the age that society considers to be *"too old,"* so you feel like your vision can no longer become a reality.

All of this might be true, but if the Lord has been telling you to *"go in your might [strength and power],"* then it definitely means that He has already empowered you to do that which He has called you to do. In order to confirm this for yourself, you need to be real about the weaknesses you perceive, and allow His peace to clear your mind of the things you thought you knew about yourself and your circumstances. The fact that God said to Gideon, *'Go in your strength'* means that Gideon already had the strength He needed to get the job done. He already had the power that would be required to complete his God-given assignment. Gideon was not able to see this power because he was so focused on the areas of his life where he felt weak. When

God gives us vision, He also equips us with the capacity to make it a reality.

You may not be the best in all areas of life; no one is since we're all imperfect, but when it comes to this vision, when it comes to this kingdom assignment, you do have the ability to bring it to life. Your weaknesses, fears, doubts, and mistakes are nothing compared to the power that is inside you. You may feel weak but God will be with you, and the Holy Spirit will provide you with the power you need to break generational curses and the cycles of addiction, poverty, and sickness if that is what you need to bring your vision to life. The enemies you are up against, the powers that the enemy uses to keep you subdued and petrified, will be destroyed. You'll discover the strength to end that toxic relationship, complete the courses, try for a baby one more time, put those business plans into action, or complete that manuscript. You'll discover the strength to do whatever you need to in order for you to show up as the woman that you have visualized once you partner with the power of peace. Finding peace where you are now will make it easier for God to reveal the strength that has been placed inside of you.

Your past will remain your past; the mistakes you made will not be removed from history; it is what it is. You may feel that you cannot play a part in starting that new initiative that will provide education to the youths in your community, but you can. Whatever you see yourself doing, you are the right woman for the job. You can do it!

Peace Provides Courage

After receiving the peace of God, Gideon had to help get rid of a few things in his town that were in direct opposition to the power of God. The people had built an altar to an idol, and the Lord gave him instructions on how to demolish it. Gideon once again became fearful because he did not want the people who had gotten fond of this idol to see what he was up to and attack him, but he wanted to regain control of his Kingdom territory, and he knew that the only way to do that was to carry out the Lord's wishes. This desire enabled him to become strategic in how he would carry out the mission.

Before you can start carrying out your mission, there may be some things in your life that you need to demolish; maybe habits that you need to break or people you may need to let go of. You should also be prepared to deal with people who may not be too happy about you disrupting the flow of things. It certainly will not be easy, but with the power of peace, you'll unlock the courage you need to carry out your plans. If you want to carry out your vision and be the new woman you know in your heart you can be, then the old things that have been holding you back will have to go. Please don't misunderstand me, the process is not about achieving perfection but rather about eliminating the things that are hindering your progress. After all, growth requires sacrifice.

Gideon understood that the people around him would not understand what he was about to do and why he was doing it. They were just fine with the way things were, and he knew they would be angry if they saw him doing what the Lord had told him to do. He was afraid of their reaction but that did not stop him. He had been given the power of peace, and with that power came the assurance from God that he would be protected. It is the same for you as you start your mission. God will be with you; you'll be able to use the power that you have been given, and you will not fail.

Because he was not fixing his eyes on the distress brought by fear but instead chose to focus on the peace that God had provided, Gideon was able to make a calculated decision in order to proceed at a more advantageous time. Instead of canceling the plan and returning to his normal life when fear came creeping, Gideon made a decision to change his tactic, and he went during the night. You don't have to face your opponents head-on to win. Sometimes God will have you go at a time when they are least expecting it, and sometimes He will have you carry out His instructions silently in order to ensure your success and protection. The execution of your vision might require you to take part in covert missions; you might need to be up late at night working while everyone else is still asleep. Just be obedient to the direction that comes from the power of peace and you'll be victorious.

Peace helps you to dominate fear by showing you that there is always more than one way to get things done. If you have a task to complete and you feel anxious about the execution, just stop, breath, and allow the power of peace to reveal the best strategy. Don't be too quick to believe that if things are not done the way others do it, then it will not work out. God knows what your experiences and circumstances are, so He will provide a strategy to suit those circumstances. It doesn't matter if others did it one way; God can help you to find a unique path that works best for you. In the pursuit of your vision, you have to be able to find the courage to switch things up.

Peace Enables Focus

If you struggle with anxiety, you will know that it is not easy to achieve peace. It's so easy to slip into days, even months, and worst years, constantly worrying about basically everything. The power of peace doesn't guarantee the absence of or total eradication of anxiety, worry, or fear. Having peace just means that when those things do come to the forefront of your thoughts, trying to derail your life, you'll be in a better place mentally, emotionally and spiritually to deal with them. It means that you'll be able to make logical decisions. Peace is the catalyst of focus.

With the power of peace, you can remain confident about your own path and maintain focus when what you are doing doesn't make sense to others. You'll not chase the things that other people have, compare your progress to that of others, and be blinded by other people's vision. Instead, you'll know to stay on the course that God has laid out for you, and you'll have the courage to do what you were created to do in spite of what people have to say about your decision to change the norm.

Woman Of The House

The Bible clearly states that the man (the husband) was created to be the head of the household. As the head, he is to be compassionate with his woman (his wife), lead in the decision making, and help to provide for his family.

As Godly women and ladies with power, we must accept the order that God has established and recognize that our role is to submit to the man (husband) who receives direction on how to sustain the family solely from God. We must wholeheartedly acknowledge and agree with God's plan and intention to set the man as the head of the household, and as we grow higher in Him, we must remain humble and always accept the will of God.

That being said, unfortunately, there are times when the man of the house doesn't operate in the way that God has instructed. The man described in Ephesians 5 and 1 Peter 3 doesn't always show up. At times things start off on a good note, but along the way, changes occur. Sometimes we start a family with a man who turned out to be one described in 1 Timothy 5:8. What do we do when the man has forfeited his role? As women, how do we proceed when who we thought was a man ready to be the man of the house just turned out to be someone content with living like one of the children?

If you started a family with a man who you thought would take up his duties but realize that he doesn't have a clue what it means to be the man of the house, then you can do one of two things; stay and work things out or leave. I cannot tell you which to choose; that is a decision you'll have to make on your own after assessing the details of your vision and seeking clarity from God. In the meantime, I know you can make peace with your situation, make peace with what is happening, acknowledge your strength, make your plans, and trust that the power you possess will give you the courage to make whatever decision you think is best. You can rely on the strength that comes from the power of peace within you to get you through your situation and provide for you and your family regardless of the outcome.

Regardless of what the outcome will be, you can take up your role as the woman of the house and submit to the ultimate, everlasting man of the house, God Himself. You are the woman of the house whether a man is present or not. Though it is frustrating, discouraging, and overwhelmingly burdensome when there is a man present and you still have to be doing everything alone, if a man is unavailable, whether it be physically, emotionally, spiritually or financially, you should not concede to hopelessness. You have the power to make things happen with or without a man. Would you prefer to have someone who will step up to his responsibility? Of course! But if it is not possible, then don't allow worry and stress to keep your mind corroded and prevent you from moving forward with pursing your vision. It will not be easy but it is possible to make peace with your circumstances and focus on moving forward. You can choose to say, "You know what, things are not the way I wish they would be, but all hope is not lost. I have a vision, and the Man who gave it to me will help me to achieve it. Things are not the best, and I wish I had help from this person, but I have divine support, and that is all I need to carry me through. Whatever decision I make regarding my situation after I have allowed peace to clear my mind will not cost me my vision."

You should also be aware that the appointment of the man (husband) as the head doesn't mean you are powerless and incapable of leading on your own. If you have to leave an abusive relationship or become a single mother in order to start showing up as your highest self, then you can do it. You'll never walk alone. Things will be different and might even be a little more challenging at first, but God is saying, *"Don't be afraid, you won't die."* (see Judges 6:23). Go in the strength you have been given. The change will not destroy you. If you have been given the confirmation to leave and you are fearful of starting over and being on your own, then know that all will be fine. Yes, it might be hard at first, and adjusting will be uncomfortable, but peace will give you the strength you need to make it work. My mother always says that when it comes to running a household, one hand cannot clap, which basically means that when two people come together and each can pull their own weight in the family, it will be a bit easier to create a stable household. This might be true, but if it is just you in this season, then snap your fingers in the meantime. A sound is produced either way; you can still create stability; you just have to be more strategic.

If the man is not stepping up, then you have the power to step up for yourself. As a matter of fact, you are required to step up for yourself nonetheless.

God will not leave you to fend for yourself. Let Him give you the power to lead as the woman of the house. If your marriage did not go as planned and you are now left without a man, just know that you are still capable of making life work. The same is true if you are a single mother. Finding peace will help you to accept your situation. Accepting your situation will give you the patience to remain calm and gradually take the steps needed to build the life you desire.

Now, if you know that the Lord is telling you to remain where you are, then continue to pray that your man will reclaim his position in the household. Pray for the strength to remain focused in your role and stay put. Pray for the strength to shake things up and create a new regime in your family. There are instances where the man is present and is a Godly man seeking to do what is required for his family, but the enemy attacks the family by coming for him since he is the head. If you don't stand firm in your position and enforce your power, then the whole family will crumble under the attacks of the enemy. Don't cower in fear. With peace as your weapon, the enemy will not stand a chance against you as the woman of the house.

When Gideon was startled by what he had seen and the Lord was giving him peace, do you notice how He said it; "Peace!" It was spoken as a command, not a request or suggestion. When faced with fearful situations, you must declare under the authority of the Holy Spirit who lives in you. Don't be intimidated by fear and uncertainty; demand and declare peace in your life. Be bold in your declarations because you have the right to be at peace.

Still Single, Still Powerful

Oh boy, here we go again! Another author coming to talk about how I should embrace singleness and wait on the Lord and I have been doing that for 30 years now, and when will I stop being single and...

I hear you! But what else are you going to do? Let's be real. The goal is to not just be introduced to "a" man but "the" man—the man who God has been preparing for you.

What is going to happen when instead of making peace with your singleness and allowing God to prepare you for that man, you wake up every day being bitter about not being married? Do you know what is going to happen if you focus too much of your attention on this? The man you keep talking about will be busy getting to know God and preparing for his eternity, while you have done nothing to get to know God, thus forfeiting your right to eternity and the chance you have to be with a Godly man because God will not be prepared to give his Godly son to an ungodly woman He barely knows.

It is not easy when your desire is to be 'boo'd up' and show up looking all cute with coordinated outfits, but if you are still single while reading this, learn to make peace with this season. Nothing good comes from rushing to another assignment prematurely. As women of God, our main purpose is to be totally committed to our heavenly Father in every season. When all is said and done, you and that man will be standing before God, giving an account for your lives as two separate individuals (see Romans 14:12). It will not be about where you had your wedding or where you had your first date. This man will have to show how much time he gave to the development of his faith, and so will you. Don't be caught up on the Instagram and YouTube weddings. Your time will come if it is God's will. In the meantime, what have you done today to strengthen the power that lives in you? How strong is the presence of the Holy Spirit in your life right now? Has the fear of being single forever prevented you from carrying out your assignments as a single lady?

Your fear of not getting married should not prevent you from fulfilling your assignment of being single. Your vision might show you being married, but it must be on God's terms in order for it to be meaningful. One thing about fear is that it tends to generate desperation, and that is not cute. Be careful not to become bitter towards God because this can lead to desperation, which may cause you to get entangled in a relationship you have no business being in. You don't want to rush a relationship only to realize that the two of you were mated, not matched by God. It is my prayer that you will not miss out on the loving household you have envisioned because of your choice to settle for counterfeit.

The Lord is intentional, which means that He has His reasons for everything He does and doesn't do. You have to own who you are in ever season, including the ones where you don't readily get what you want. So don't go around trying to get the attention of every man you think seems like he could be right for you, instead, live with poise and composure and trust that in the right time the right one will find you.

The notion that you attract who you are is true in some sense but can be dangerous if we constantly fixate on the fact that if we attract the wrong kind of men, that automatically means we're the wrong kind of woman. Once you are walking in your power, people will be drawn to you. Think of the light bulb that captures the attention of every buzzing bug with wings. Power garners attention, which means that you'll attract the good and the bad. You'll attract men who have similar values as you and ones who don't. Your power lies in the ability to accept what you think you deserve, and you should know by now that God's daughter deserves the best.

As you remain close to God and spend time getting to know who He really is, He will show you who you are and who you are meant to be with. You'll also discover how valuable and powerful you are as a single woman.

If you make peace with who you are and what you have in this season, when the power of God is finished with you, you'll be that good thing that He promised His son, and that is when you'll be ready to be a wife. And let me just say that being "a good thing" starts with being good to, and for, the current version of you, as well as recognizing the power that you carry in your single season.

Fulfill your singleness season, and know that God has not forgotten about you. Make peace with who you are in this time of your life, and don't allow fear to overshadow the promises associated with your vision.

Someone once said that as a single woman, people will feel more comfortable asking you about your relationship status than they do asking about your Kingdom status. Put things into perspective for yourself. Don't allow people to rush your process; take your time and stay close to God. That is one way to guarantee that you'll be showing up as your highest self in your marriage when the time is right.

Accepting who you are and recognizing that you are still powerful in this season will help you to deal with the hurtful comments from people who don't really understand who you are and what you are about.

Ways to dominate fear with the Power of Peace:

- Release the fear from your mind through your mouth so that it can reach God's ears.
- Remind yourself that you already have the strength to do what is required of you.
- Boldly command peace over your situation daily.
- Learn when to implement alternative measures as you carry out your plans.
- Navigate each season of life patiently.
- Be patient with yourself throughout the process.

The Power of Prayer

Don't be anxious about anything, but in every situation, by prayer and petition, with thanksgiving, present your requests to God. And the peace of God, which transcends all understanding, will guard your hearts and your minds in Christ Jesus.
Philippians 4:6-7 (NIV)

Prayer Reveals Your Desires

God is omniscient; He knows every thought you ever had and you'll ever have. He sees everything that goes on in your daily life, and He knows what you need in order for you to live the life that you want. In spite of all that, He still wants you to ask Him for the things you want and need. We're all given free will, which means that we really don't have to go to Him in our times of need if we don't want to, but He wants us to do so because He wants us to make our desires known to Him. Basically, He wants us to want Him to help. The Lord doesn't want puppets who only come to Him because He made them do it. He wants you to willingly approach Him with your requests because you know that He is the only one who can help you to achieve the desires that you possess.

Because God is omniscient, He would have already had your item set aside for when you decide to ask for it. If you choose not to, then that is up to you. Sometimes we complain to ourselves and wonder if God doesn't see what is happening in our lives. We say, "Doesn't He see that I need money to pay for university? Isn't it obvious that my family needs to be unified? Why doesn't He do anything? Can't He see that I'm terrified of starting this venture? Why doesn't He help me?" Instead of talking about God in situations like this, try talking to Him. Tell Him what you want, and that is how He will be able to help. Sit with Him in the quiet of the morning or reach out to Him in the hustle and bustle of the day, whatever works for you. He's always listening.

If it is healing you need, ask for it. If you want to change your life and you are not sure where to start, ask Him to help you. Make your desires known to Him through prayer and He will hear you and help you.

Prayer Causes Miracles

When we pray, God moves. You can actually persuade God to change the course of your life and allow things to work in your favour when you ask for what you want by praying the way you know how to. A miracle is *an extraordinary and welcome event that is not explicable by natural or scientific laws and is therefore attributed to a divine agency*. The Lord is omnipresent; He exists everywhere at the same time. Don't ask me how, I have no idea, but I believe this with every fiber of my being because of my own experiences with the miracles of God. I was in Jamaica, prayed for the protection of a cousin in another country, and God came through. When you ask God for what you want, you'll be able to receive divine support wherever you are and for whoever you want. The power of prayer that you possess can be used as a shield for whoever you direct it to. You could be deep in the belly of a large fish or in a palace surrounded by danger, and God will show up for you just as He did for Jonah and Esther.

I think we're often hesitant to use the power of prayer because we don't believe in the authority that we have been given to use it. With the power you have been given, you have the right to challenge every threat made against your vision and purpose. Don't be intimidated by the attacks that are made against you; the words that flow from your mouth through the power of the Holy Spirit are like daggers to the devices of the enemy. It doesn't matter how you ended up between a rock and a hard place and who is out to harm you. Whether you are facing opposition at work, in your ministry, or in your family, prayer can turn things around. Whether you pray in the presence of others or alone in your own space, God will hear you because He cares about you. If God, the divine agent, is for you, then it doesn't matter who is against you, you are safe. It is all good; don't even worry about it. He changes things that seem unchangeable. He can manipulate any situation on your behalf, whether man-made or not.

When you find yourself in a life-altering situation and there is no one around who can help, don't be afraid because you are never defenseless. When others around you are too stunned or are too terrified themselves to come to your aid, you can count on the power of prayer to deliver you from harm's way.

The miracle you seek can be achieved through prayer. Sometimes we end up in difficult situations as a result of our own disobedience or because we fail to heed the warning from others. We may also end up being burdened down because of our inability to turn our backs on sin and live the life that we're called to live. Likewise, we may passionately pursue our vision and end up at a roadblock, unable to see a way forward. Before you know it, in comes fear, doubt, and anxiety to persuade you to give up and convince you that you were never good enough to carry out your plans anyway.

The fear of letting God down can affect our ability to move forward sometimes. The fear that He no longer loves us or that we don't love Him enough because of our inability to be obedient can also cause us to give up during difficult times. When we pray for the ability to dominate fear and seek God's forgiveness and direction, He doesn't pull up our past mistakes with the intention of rejecting us if He sees a major offense. Even though He requires obedience and we often get ourselves in sticky situations because we simply don't heed His warnings, He doesn't hold it against us and withholds His helpful hand when we ask for it. He is not going to withhold your miracle because of mistakes you made in the past. Miracles are not for those who only live a perfect life; they are for those who recognize the power of the Holy Spirit in them and the potential they have to transform any situation through prayer.

God delights in every story we choose to tell Him. He never gets annoyed at any question we ask Him, and with every mistake we make, He will show up every time we ask Him for help to fix it. This is not to say we have full range to abuse the power of prayer and take God's grace for granted.

There is no moment that is too intense for God; there is no pit He cannot lift us from; and no wound He cannot heal. When you are facing the consequences of your mistakes and are on the verge of total despair, when you have nowhere left to run and when you feel hopeless, fearful, and alone, when you feel like you are forgotten, and there is no one else around to help you, God's intervention is only a prayer away.

Regardless of where you are in life physically, mentally, emotionally, or financially, God can help you to transform your life and set you on a new path. He can be moved to demolish your fears. That is how powerful your prayer is.

Wordless Prayers Are Still Powerful

Now there are also those moments when words cannot describe how we feel, and we cannot audibly ask for our miracle. I mean, those moments when the pain is so hard to bear and you try so hard to find the right words to explain to God exactly what you are feeling and exactly what you want from Him, but the only sound you are able to produce are mumbling between sobs. Well, He speaks every language, including blubber and gibberish, so God will not miss a thing. Your prayers are powerful even when they don't seem to be making sense (see Romans 8:26). See, sister, He thinks of everything and is so interested in what you have to say that He makes the effort to figure it out. *Boy oh boy, do we wish that all men were like that!*

God sees beyond the mess and provides miracles in spite of it. When you pray for your miracle, the power behind it terminates everything that might try to stop it from happening. When you pray, God moves; it is that simple. He moves in ways that we may never understand. He softens hearts, alters the decisions of others, and manipulates events and situations on our behalf when we pray. Have you ever been in a situation where someone is trying to take all the credit for something you received? Little did they know how much you prayed! Yes, he or she might have played a vital role in the outcome, but you know that things would have gone differently if you did not talk to God about it. Still, don't even get me started on what can happen when you and all your powerful sisters come together and pray. Fear would not know what hit it until it was too late.

When we pray, we go to war with forces that rise against us; that includes fear. We know that in our own strength, we're powerless to the attacks of the enemy, but through prayer, we can win. The devil often uses those around us to discourage us and make us feel less than we really are, and we sometimes develop a fear of proving them right. We listen to the negative things that people say about us; those words that say we will not be victorious in our pursuits, we will never amount to anything, and that we will always be in the depressive state that we're in because that is how our family members were so that is all we will ever be. Well, you have the power to cancel, reverse, denounce and demolish all of that.

All the negativity and deadly prophecies bred from jealousy, hate, and ignorance are annulled when you pray. It may be hard to tell that God is fighting for you because our prayers don't always get answered immediately, but trust me, even when you cannot see it, God is at work.

Pray In Your Own Way

Don't be daunted by the prayers of others around you; utilize your own unique prayer power. Sometimes we feel insecure because our prayers are not as loud or eloquently articulated as others. The power doesn't reside in the volume of your voice when you pray; it is all in your sincerity and authority, as well as your trust in God's ability to deliver what you have prayed for.

Luke 10:19 says: *"Behold, I give unto you power to tread on serpents and scorpions, and over all the power of the enemy: and nothing shall by any means hurt you." (KJV)*. Some translations say, *"I give you authority to trample over all powers of the enemy."*
This means you have been given a position in the Kingdom of God that comes with a power that can destroy those of the enemy. While this authority leads to the boldness that can produce ear-piercing prayers, if you pray silently on earth, the forces against you will hear them loud and clear.

So when you are faced with the power of fear and all other powers of evil, you can be confident in your authority. Don't concede to defeat when you have the definitive power living in you. Don't allow the powers of the enemy to have a say in what happens to you in life. You have the power to stop the attacks on your life. You have the power to stop the attacks on the lives of your loved ones. You will not be killed by the powers that are rising up against you. Fear can't kill you when you choose to strengthen and apply the power of prayer in your life. Pray with your own power, and don't be intimidated by the prayer of others.

Something Else

We're not going to receive everything that we pray for. If you have been taught anything contrary to this, then you have been deceived. Unfortunately, that is just not how this faith-walk works. Our purpose comes with a few promises and a few perks. While God will definitely come through on His promises and give us a few perks because of our obedience and faithfulness to Him, He is not going to provide everything that we desire.

When we ask God for the things we desire, the answer *"no"* is not what we want to hear, and *"wait"* can be just as frustrating; trust me, I have had my share of those. Those are the most heartbreaking and disappointing responses. God's love is unconditional, and He can see everything concerning your life. This means that because of His love, the things that He has planned for your life will ultimately end up being things that you and others around you will enjoy. Also, know that the things that God provides will help bring glory to His name, not yours. They will bring people, including you, to Him, not cause them to stray.

Sometimes the things we desire are truly not good for us and can potentially lead us astray. That is why as you chase your vision, you should be in constant prayer so as not to end up chasing something that was never meant for you. The answers we receive from God when we pray are for our own good. When it feels as if you are praying and God is not doing anything or providing what you have asked for, just know that He is still busy doing something else. You might not receive the things you ask for, but if you trust and keep believing that God heard you and wait patiently, then you'll be pleasantly surprised to realize that He was silently preparing something more than you ever imagined. We think we know what we need, but we don't always know. God knows how to read between the lines and still come through even if you did not quite ask for what He was expecting you to.

We might put a limit on the things we ask for, but there is no limit on the things that God can provide. So when you modestly ask for the little that you desire in that moment, God will always bless you with the bounty you deserve. Don't give up on your prayer life because you have not received the answer you were hoping for. The power of prayer is still alive in you, and it is working even if you don't see it.

Don't allow the fear of missing out to discourage you when you don't get the things that appear to be associated with status and prosperity.

Find peace in the knowledge that God has your best interest at heart, and He will never overlook you. Maintain your peace so that fear doesn't rush you into taking actions that will cost you your promise.

"This kind can come out only by prayer."

"And one of the multitude answered and said, Master, I have brought unto thee my son, which hath a dumb spirit; And wheresoever he taketh him, he teareth him: and he foameth, and gnasheth with his teeth, and pineth away: and I spake to thy disciples that they should cast him out; and they could not." (Mark 9:17-18 - KJV).

When Jesus saw that the people came running together, he rebuked the foul spirit, saying unto him, Thou dumb and deaf spirit, I charge thee, come out of him, and enter no more into him. And the spirit cried, and rent him sore, and came out of him: and he was as one dead; insomuch that many said, He is dead. But Jesus took him by the hand, and lifted him up; and he arose. And when he was come into the house, his disciples asked him privately, Why could not we cast him out? And he said unto them, This kind can come forth by nothing, but by prayer and fasting. (Mark 9:25-29 - KJV).

Be mindful of momentary prayer. This is prayer that is done only when we want something from God, when there is no daily interaction. Imagine having a friend who you cherish and want to talk to every day, but the only time this friend talks to you is when he or she needs something from you. That is the same as talking to God only when we have an issue.

Daily prayer strengthens the bond between you and God. The strength of your relationship impacts the effectiveness of the power that lies within you. Some of you are dealing with serious issues that only prayer and fasting can address. When fear and anxiety become a stronghold, we need the power of the Holy Spirit to remove [break] it.

Jesus spent hours in the presence of God, learning from Him and gaining the strength [power] He needed to fight against the powers of the enemy and accomplish His mission. In order to dominate the power of fear in our daily lives, we must spend each day strengthening the power within us, and one way to do that is through prayer. If you are serious about executing your vision, then you have to get serious about prayer. Get a prayer journal, and create a prayer plan with specific things you need to ask God for and about. You can never pray too much when you are attempting to dominate fear.

When Jesus went up against the impure spirit, He did not make a suggestion for it to leave; He commanded it to leave because His prayer life gave Him the confidence to demand what He needed with boldness and authority. When we develop the power of prayer, and we understand the authority we possess, we don't just ask for our healing and deliverance, we command everything that is opposing it to leave.

Resistance Through Prayer

"Submit yourselves therefore to God. Resist the devil, and he will flee from you." (James 4:7 - KJV).

This passage of scripture doesn't only apply to temptation; resisting the devil is about rejecting everything he stands for and every power he brings. Your resistance is a total defiance of the plans and schemes that the enemy tries to trap and destroy you with. To resist is to use your power to counteract these plans or defeat the powers rising up against you. Your prayer is a magnificent form of resistance. When you pray, you are basically refusing to bend to the will of the enemy by choosing to focus all your energy on God. When you pray, you are refusing to allow fear to control your life. Prayer is a form of submission that gives God permission to fight for you. When you pray, you are actively turning away from the enemy and the fears, doubts, addictions, anger, and anxieties that he brings up against you. It is like you are saying, *"I hear what you're saying, and I see what you're trying to do, but I don't agree with it; I don't accept it."*

"I know you want to kill my purpose, but I'm not having it."

"I'm struggling financially right now, and you are trying to get me to believe that I will live in poverty for the rest of my life, but God has given me a promise, and I will work hard and believe Him for it."

"You want my children to be disobedient and stray from my teachings and God's path but not today, Satan!"

"My marriage is good, and I know in my heart that this is a kingdom union and you want to create discord and separation, but I will resist this plan."

"I am going to challenge these schemes of yours, and when I do, you have to fall!"

When you resist the powers of the enemy, they flee, so pray with your power. Depression flees when you pray, fear flees when you pray, anger, addiction, and feelings of unworthiness flee when you pray. Antibodies help our bodies to resist infections, and prayer gives us power so we can fight against the powers of the enemy.

So pray.

The Power of Faith

"He said to her, "Daughter, your faith has healed you. Go in peace and be freed from your suffering."
Mark 5:34 (NIV)

In order to experience a life filled with power, we must be willing to look beyond what we can see with our physical eyes. When we get accustomed to sorrow, it is not easy to believe we can experience joy. When you are bombarded with feelings of fear, it is difficult to understand how to carry out the plans that will lead to the completion of your vision. When we go through life facing poverty and loss, it is not easy to believe we can receive kingdom wealth. When we or our loved ones get sick, and we're accustomed to suffering and despair, it is not easy to believe in the power of Faith.

Faith challenges us to shift our focus from our physical circumstances, reject what we know to be true and rely on God's spoken promises. Now, of course, faith alone cannot bring about change; our actions also play a major role in the process.

Get In Position

In the book of Mark, we're introduced to a woman who for twelve years had identified as the sick woman who only got worse instead of better. While Jesus was on His way to answering someone's request, she heard about Him. This woman decided to see Jesus with the hope of being healed. No one had to tell her to go, and Jesus did not call her Himself. She heard about Him, saw an opportunity to seek Him, and since she had tried everything else she could possibly think of, she decided that she would not allow Him to leave without trying one last time. She had a vision for her life, and she was convinced that Jesus could help her to make it a reality.

I can just imagine how unworthy she must have felt; how timid and afraid of being rejected by not only Jesus but others around Him who must have known about her struggles. Despite this, without calling any attention to herself, she still reached out and just touched His clothes, thinking that that would be enough to heal her.

The Power of Faith

Imagine the courage this must have taken. She could have given up and allowed the devil to convince her that all those other attempts to cure her in the past had failed, so this time would not be any different. But she pushed beyond her former experiences and focused on what she believed could happen. In that moment of faith, she got herself in the right position, touched His clothes, and was completely healed. As you battle with your own fears and strive to become the woman of your dreams, just know that faith can bring an end to suffering.

After she touched Jesus, she immediately felt in her body that she was healed. Everything within her that was causing her to be sick just dried up, and at that moment, Jesus turned around and asked His disciples who touched His clothes. He knew that someone had touched Him because He had realized that *"power had gone out from Him."* (v. 30). You have to pull out that power for yourself. There is already a call; the Holy Spirit is already present in your life, and all you need to do to obtain the power that can get you to the place you desire is to reach out and grab it.

As long as you have breath in your lungs, you have the opportunity to receive the power that can get you to where you want to be. Nothing can separate you from that power. Now I know I said that desperation is not cute, but when it comes to you fighting for the fulfillment of your purpose on earth, you really cannot afford to be cute. When it comes to you dominating the fear that has hindered your progress, you certainly cannot afford to stay still.

Imagine that this is your one chance to receive your breakthrough, and the enemy is trying to push you back with fear and depression. Forget the people around you who don't understand that the thing you need from Jesus is the only thing that will help you to feel fulfilled and excited about life. Don't listen to people whose own fears and disbelief are trying to get you to walk away from your chance to start your business, go to therapy, or adopt your child. They don't understand the level of faith you have in God, and that is okay. They don't understand why you are so desperate to receive the power from Jesus, and that is okay. Receive the power you need to move past fear by getting yourself in the position to see, hear from and talk to God. Go to church if you need to, study the Word of God if you need to, pray when you need to and exercise your faith when you need to.

It doesn't matter if you have been struggling with fear for twelve years or twelve seconds; the struggles could be a result of your experiences or something you just always had in you. Once you are in the presence of Jesus, you are able to receive His power. His power is your power, and your power can make you well; your power of faith will make you well.

Step out of your hiding place; you have been there long enough. Don't allow fear to keep you from doing what you know you were called to do. Don't allow fear to keep you trapped in a life that doesn't bring you joy. Make yourself known to the Lord so that His power can be placed inside of you. If your fears will not move, you'll have to move with them and believe that the power you have received will sustain you.

Vision Over Sight

Jesus was on His way to tend to a little girl when the woman we spoke about earlier reached out to Him.

"While Jesus was still speaking, some people came from the house of Jairus, the synagogue leader. "Your daughter is dead," they said. "Why bother the teacher anymore?" Overhearing what they said, Jesus told him, "Don't be afraid; just believe." He did not let anyone follow him except Peter, James and John the brother of James. When they came to the home of the synagogue leader, Jesus saw a

commotion, with people crying and wailing loudly. He went in and said to them, "Why all this commotion and wailing? The child is not dead but asleep." But they laughed at him. After he put them all out, he took the child's father and mother and the disciples who were with him, and went in where the child was. He took her by the hand and said to her, "Talitha koum!" (which means "Little girl, I say to you, get up!"). Immediately the girl stood up and began to walk around (she was twelve years old). At this they were completely astonished." (Mark 5:35-42 - NIV).

People who don't understand your vision will always question your actions as you strive to pursue it. The things you may be able to see as a result of your faith will not be apparent to others. Therefore, you may be constantly told that the things you seek will never become a reality. What would have happened if the opinions of others caused Jairus to give up on his faith? They told him that his little girl was dead and that nothing would be done to save her. Jesus told him not to be afraid because she was only sleeping.

The report of the Lord is the only one that matters. So when it comes to the fulfillment of the dream that you have been given, who will you believe? If you choose to believe the report of the Lord in this matter, then you have to be prepared to be laughed at by others. It is okay though because you know that you'll be having the last laugh when what you believed God for finally becomes a reality.

When you show up in that industry that you were created to thrive in, be prepared to be laughed at and overlooked by the people around you who cannot understand why you are there. As a matter of fact, you need to beat them to it and just have a laugh at yourself for how incredibly insane this vision of yours appears to be considering your current situation. You need to have that conversation with yourself.

Lady With Power

Talk to yourself right now and get all the laughs out of the way in preparation for what people might say.

Since you might be fearful of facing ridicule from others, let's put that fear to shame by getting the laughs out now. It might seem ridiculous, but preparing for the possibility of fearful and humiliating encounters can do wonders to alleviate stress and provide the courage to go through with your plans.

_____ *(Your Name)*, you have got to be out of your mind for thinking that you can

_____
_____
_____
_____
_____ *(Your Vision)*.

Are you laughing yet?

I mean,

_____
_____
_____
_____
_____ *(Your explanation as to why the vision is unfathomable. For example, "you are from a poor family, you are too old or you don't have the proper education and resources")*.

Now that you have gotten a good laugh at how huge your vision is compared to what you think you are capable of, the enemy cannot use anything to actually get you to give up. Do this as many times as you need to so that if you happen to face mockery from others, you can go right ahead and laugh with them while you continue to pursue your vision. It doesn't matter what you or others can see; what matters is the vision that God gave you and the level at which you believe Him.

Put Them All Out

You know what you want out of this encounter with Jesus. The power that He possesses is now living in you, and you know and believe what it can do. In order for the power of faith to be activated and break the hold that fear, sickness, or pain has on you, you'll need to let certain things and people go. You have to go to war with everything that is against your vision.

People around you may say your vision can never work; you don't have the money, your window of opportunity has closed, you are too old. They might say, "Girl, why are you wasting your prayers on this? This will never work out." Try to limit the time you spend interacting with people who don't encourage your efforts to create a better life for yourself. Step out in faith and leave all the mess behind. Leave the naysayers who will cause you to doubt. Put out the people who would rather have you waste your days gossiping about what everyone else is doing instead of preparing; the same people who would rather drag you away, instead of lead you to the place where Jesus is. Essentially, put out the ones who will feed your fear.

I am not telling you to be disrespectful or allow the knowledge of your power to get to your head and start cutting everyone off. You'll need people on your journey, we all do. Jesus brought Peter, James, and John when He was on His way to help Jairus. You have to know who to bring on your mission and let everyone else stay outside. Ladies with power know how to *put them all out* with class, clarity, confidence, and humility.

You'll know who to let in on your vision. These are the people who will add to your faith and who you know you can count on to pray for you when you are having hard times in life. These are the people who will encourage you when you feel like giving up, but even if you are the only one with radical faith and you have to go on your own with Jesus by your side, then you have enough.

Aside from negative people, your own characteristics might be at war with the power of faith in you. Release unforgiveness, let go of the anger and bitterness you are harbouring. Put them all out and get to work on your plans to become the woman in your vision. You cannot go higher with unnecessary baggage weighing you down.

The power you possess cannot work in hate, malice, jealousy, spite, and greed. You have to be real with yourself and be willing to admit when these attributes are not only coming from the people around you. The powers of the enemy tend to work as a team; these qualities can also increase fear. You'll need to do a power check to see if these opposing powers are working in you.

Belief For Unbelief

Even now, you are probably wrestling with disbelief. You probably want to believe that things can change for you, but you are thinking, "How can everything that is happening in my life right now turn into something good?"

It is really difficult to exchange worry for worship and keep a high spirit in perilous times. You should not feel guilty for having doubt; having faith in God doesn't mean that you'll be entirely without unbelief.

It is also really difficult to keep the faith going when it seems as if you are in a cycle of bad breaks, rejection, and disappointments. Don't give up. It is not easy, but God promises to be with you every step of the way. When disappointments happen, weep if you need to, there is no shame in that, but don't give up on God's ability to make things happen for you. When you feel your faith dwindling, ask Him to help you keep just a tiny bit so you can keep going. It is okay to move with unbelief.

The Power of Preparation

"Give me six hours to chop down a tree and I will spend the first four sharpening the axe."
—**Abraham Lincoln**

Visualize, Prepare, Show up

Preparation is the action or process of making something ready for use or service or of getting ready for some occasion, test, or duty. Once you have identified what you want to achieve in life, the next step is to prepare for it. If you want to show up with impact, then you most definitely cannot overlook the preparation process.

Let's say, for instance, your goals require you to make a career change; your preparation process should include signing up for classes and purchasing the materials you'll need to study and pass your exams. This process should also include strategies on how to improve your mindset as you prepare to level up.

The preparation process will help to provide you with a clear understanding of why you are pursuing your goal. Visualizing is essential; however, identifying your "why" will keep you motivated during setbacks. The process will also make it easy for you to set relevant objectives. While your goals may be time-consuming, it is very important that you pace yourself while you prepare. If you over-exert yourself and end up being burnt, you will not be able to enjoy the fruits of your labour. As time passes, you might develop a fear of not being able to complete your goals before getting older. Take your time; everything is going according to plan.

You can spend an entire day working and not be productive. In other words, you can spend several hours doing several tasks and end up realizing that not only did you fail to complete one, but they were all done incorrectly. You would then need to spend even more time doing them all over again. The truth is, multitasking doesn't always lead to productivity and can increase your anxiety. As you prepare, utilize wisdom and spend time on the things that are essential to your goals.

Create a system that can allow you to finish your tasks effectively without causing too much physical stress. Learn to delegate or ask other people's opinion.

Preparing helps you to acquire the right supplies that you will need. It also helps you to manage your time and resources wisely and identify and implement solutions for potential problems. The process helps to build confidence which reduces fear, anxiety, and stress. When you prepare for the best and anticipate the worst things that can happen, you are able to calmly perform the task at hand. The 'viral culture' can make it seem as if things just always happen overnight. While technology has made it a bit easier to achieve success, we will still need to make adequate preparation as it relates to certain things. Preparation also builds commitment, confidence, resilience, and determination, qualities you will need as you move towards your vision.

As you make your plans, try to guard against using preparation as an excuse to procrastinate. Did you know that your fears can cause you to sub-consciously procrastinate? In your mind, you want to ensure that everything is perfect before you actually start to do something on your list. However, in reality, you are actually afraid that you will fail if you try, so you are prolonging the process as long as you can.

Preparation doesn't guarantee success; things don't always go as planned, and that is fine. We will not be able to control everything in life. Try not to think about failure as a representation of who you are. Instead, think of it as an exciting adventure that allows you to push your limits and find ways to discover surprising secrets about yourself and how you can live your life. Failing in one venture doesn't mean that you will fail in all. Sometimes failure is needed in order to provide the knowledge required to succeed in the next endeavor.

So if you happen to visualize, prepare, show up and fail, don't give up.

Stay Ready

Always be ready for the power of fear. Fear is one of the enemy's weapons that is used to hinder the actions you need to take in order for you to fulfill your purpose. He will always try to kill your vision, so you need to always be ready to defend it. You cannot show up on the battlefield unprepared and unarmed. That is a guaranteed way to be defeated. The power of fear is a mighty weapon, but you now know that the power of God is mightier, and when you always keep your guard up, you will always be ready to defend your territories.

Consider the following scriptures as you think about how you can be on your guard for when fear shows up:

2 Corinthians 10:4-5 (KJV)
(For the weapons of our warfare are not carnal, but mighty through God to the pulling down of strong holds;) Casting down imaginations, and every high thing that exalteth itself against the knowledge of God, and bringing into captivity every thought to the obedience of Christ;

Ephesians 6:10-18 (NIV)
Finally, be strong in the Lord and in his mighty power. Put on the full armor of God, so that you can take your stand against the devil's schemes. For our struggle is not against flesh and blood, but against the rulers, against the authorities, against the powers of this dark world and against the spiritual forces of evil in the heavenly realms. Therefore, put on the full armor of God, so that when the day of evil comes, you may be able to stand your ground, and after you have done everything, to stand. Stand firm then, with the belt of truth buckled around your waist, with the breastplate of righteousness in place, and with your feet fitted with the readiness that comes from the gospel of peace. In addition to all this, take up the shield of faith, with which you

can extinguish all the flaming arrows of the evil one. Take the helmet of salvation and the sword of the Spirit, which is the word of God. And pray in the Spirit on all occasions with all kinds of prayers and requests. With this in mind, be alert and always keep on praying for all the Lord's people.

The weapons you need to win the power struggle and execute your vision might not be visible, but this doesn't mean they are weak. You may think that because the power of fear shows up so strong in your life, you will not be able to overpower it. That is a lie! No matter how overwhelmed you might be in fearful situations, the armour of God is a great protector and can defend you against any attack.

Be careful not to allow weak spots to develop in your armour. Fit your feet with the gospel of peace daily; take up the shield of faith daily; take up the helmet of salvation and the sword of the Spirit daily; and pray in the spirit daily. Stand firm in truth daily, and set the breastplate of righteousness in place daily. Don't be afraid of the enemy's advances. Instead, do everything you can in anticipation of these advances so that you will not be caught off guard.

Imagine what would happen to the sword of a warrior who did not spend the time to check on it periodically. It would eventually get dull and even rusty, right? If this warrior is called upon in a time of spontaneous war, his sword would be useless.

You cannot afford to be caught off guard while you are heading towards your vision. Even when you don't feel like doing it, refer to the instructions listed in Ephesians even as you make tangible preparations. Even when you are not sure what you are preparing for when you feel the urge to pray, pray. If you get the urge to read the Word, then do it. The Holy Spirit will sometimes try to warn you when the enemy is going to attack, so when you *'get a feeling',* roll with it.

Always be ready to fulfill your purpose. Having a growth mindset is key to your readiness as you strive to fulfill your purpose. With a growth mindset, you will always be doing what you can to increase your knowledge, improve your abilities and develop your ability to perform your tasks well. Because of this commitment, you will be ready to complete the assignments related to your vision and purpose, even when called upon at a moment's notice.

You don't want to miss out on opportunities God sends your way because of laziness and procrastination. If you want to be the best in your business, act like you will be audited every day. If you are trying to make it in the art world, always have your portfolio ready. If you want to hear your songs on the radio, ensure you always have a demo on you. It might seem silly but you will feel a lot sillier if you meet a producer or a gallery owner and you don't have anything to present.

Act as if at any moment life is going to give you a pop quiz related to your vision, and you don't want to fail it. This takes consistency, drive, and a hunger to make it to the place you have envisioned. The more you focus on preparing, the more you will be able to dominate your fear of failure, rejection, and ridicule. This will also help you to feel less rushed.

Jesus spent a lot of time preparing for the cross. He was always praying and fasting, and this increased His power. With this increase in power, He was always ready to heal when someone sick came along and always prepared to teach those who asked questions about the Kingdom of God. Jesus gained confidence and wisdom regarding His own vision and purpose because He spent a lot of time preparing for them.

There is a popular quote by Eleanor Roosevelt that says, "Great minds discuss ideas. Average minds discuss events. Small minds discuss people." Powerful ladies are not small-minded women who gossip about what others are building instead of making their own preparations. While others around her are building, she doesn't spend her time talking about the structure that they are developing because she realizes the more she does that, the shorter her own preparation time will be.

Don't waste your time talking about what others are doing. In the time you would have spent doing that, sis is over there with a completed mortgage application form, business plan, and doctoral dissertation. Learn from her.

Instead of gossiping about the progress that other women are making on their own vision, try to learn from them, ask questions and gain some information on how you can make your own strides. If you are on the receiving end of the gossip, don't allow that to phase you. Just keep working because it will definitely pay off in the end.

Always be ready for God's return

"Then the kingdom of heaven will be like this. Ten bridesmaids took their lamps and went to meet the bridegroom. Five of them were foolish, and five were wise. When the foolish took their lamps, they took no oil with them; but the wise took flasks of oil with their lamps. As the bridegroom was delayed, all of them became drowsy and slept. But at midnight there was a shout, 'Look! Here is the bridegroom! Come out to meet him.' Then all those bridesmaids got up and trimmed their lamps. The foolish said to the wise, 'Give us some of your oil, for our lamps are going out.' But the wise replied, 'No! there will not be enough for you and for us; you had better go to the dealers and buy some for yourselves.' And while they went to buy it, the bridegroom came, and those who were ready went with him into the wedding banquet; and the door was shut. Later the other bridesmaids came also, saying, 'Lord, lord, open to us.' But he

replied, *'Truly I tell you, I don't know you.' Keep awake therefore, for you know neither the day nor the hour."* Matthew 25:1-13 (NIV).

Potential Power: What Kind of Power do You Have?

Matthew 7:24-27 talks about two people who heard the same message but ended up doing two different things. Based on this principle, let's picture two ladies who have reached a point in their respective lives where they have saved enough money or received a loan from the National Housing Trust to build a house from scratch instead of buying one that has already been built. Being uncertain of where to start and the details involved in the process, both ladies decided to attend a seminar hosted by highly qualified architects and realtors. Each lady received the same information pamphlet and sat through the same PowerPoint presentation, and when the day was over, each left having been exposed to the same information.

Based on what she learnt about building a house and being a homeowner, the first lady decided to build her house on a solid foundation. When she finished the house and was getting settled, it started to rain. Even though the accompanying wind was beating against her brand new home, it was not destroyed. The second lady, however, decided to build her house on sand. When it began to rain, and the wind started beating against her house, everything came crashing down, leaving her without a home.

We have all heard that knowledge is power. Personally, through recent events, I have realized that it is actually potential power. Knowledge can be obtained so easily these days. With increasing access to technology, whatever we need to know can be found with a simple Google search anywhere and anytime. It is the choices we make after obtaining this information that determines the extent of the impact this knowledge can have on our lives. If we acquire the information that we seek and choose to let it stay in our brain without applying it, we merely possess knowledge and the potential to be powerful once we actually use it.

Similarly, you can know something and not truly understand or know how to apply it. In Jamaica, high school students who want to move on to the University level must first obtain the necessary grades by pursuing the dreaded Caribbean Secondary Education Certificate exams. The grades obtained in each subject depend on how well each student did in the respective profiles. These profiles range from experimental skills for the Sciences to enquiry and communication for Caribbean History and reasoning for Mathematics. There are three profiles however that are applicable to all subject areas: knowledge, comprehension, and use of knowledge.

For each student, simply knowing the formula to solve Pythagoras Theorem or knowing the anatomy of the body is just not enough when seeking to get to a higher level in their education. So, when the big day arrives, if these students didn't do all they could to ensure that they understand the material they were taught, they will not be able to confidently answer the question, which would cause them to fear the results. It is also safe to say that these results would be unsatisfactory.

It is not just about knowing; it is about what you do with the things you know. As you set out to accomplish your vision, you have to gain as much knowledge and understanding in the relevant areas to alleviate any fear of showing up unprepared.

I want to challenge you to do your research, seek understanding, make your plans and wisely apply the knowledge that you gain so you can crush fear and succeed.

The Power of Fear

"One of the greatest discoveries a man makes, one of his great surprises, is to find he can do what he was afraid he couldn't do."
— **Henry Ford**

"You can discover what your enemy fears most by observing the means he uses to frighten you."
— **Eric Hoffer**

If you made it this far in the book, you now know that despite his best efforts to prevent the execution of your vision, you possess power to overthrow the enemy. By now, you also know that you don't have to feel intimidated when going up against his set of powers, so let's talk about one of them.

Here is a list of things that fear intends to do when it shows up in your life:

1. Kill your hopes and dreams.
2. Cause you to miss out on fruitful encounters.
3. Cause you to question your ability to accomplish your goals.
4. Intimidate you.
5. Cultivate timidity and uncertainty.
6. Convince you to think you have failed before you have even started.
7. Create insecurities, stress, anxiety, health issues, unforgiveness, depression, and anger.
8. Cause you to stay in your comfort zone where you will not grow.
9. Ruin the relationship that you have with others.
10. Ultimately prevent you from executing your vision.

The enemy is trying to use fear to kill your dream. He doesn't want you to show up the way God wants you to because if you do, he will not be able to maintain the hold he has on your mind. You'll have a brand new mindset and a better understanding of the power that you possess. He knows that if you are able to see the power and the potential you have and realize how capable you are of actually making life-changing transformations, then you will start to pray and believe more.

The enemy knows that if you are able to look beyond the fear that you encounter, you will recognize he is behind it. And if you are able to see his hand in the situation, then you will be more intentional about directing all your power towards him and not the circumstances surrounding the fear. You'll demand that your finances, grades at school, creativity for business, health, and mind be released from his grasp. The power of fear and timidity will gradually be replaced with that of a clear mind (see 2 Timothy 1:7). Instead of cowering when he does something beyond your control, you will stand firm with your authority, and you will confuse him with your faith and praise.

Imagine someone making a plan that is devious and specific to what they know will upset you. What do you think will happen if you just shake your head, smile at the craziness, and go on your merry way when they execute this plan? They will get confused and wonder why you are not hurt and bothered by what they have done. They also might feel a little embarrassed that you showed them up, which could increase their anger and resentment toward you, causing them to come up with schemes that are even more sinister.

That is the enemy you are up against. That is what the one causing your fear is like. When you expose him, then it will be a lot easier to dominate fear. In this day and age, the enemy is doing all he can to paint himself in another light by using culture, songs, and movies. He is using the content that we're exposed to, to cast himself as relatable and deserving of sympathy. He wants us to be tricked into seeing him differently; as charming, down-to-earth, sexy and funny. He wants us to think that he is harmless, that the weapons we have been instructed to use against him are pointless and unnecessary.

There are churches that no longer use the term "the enemy" because they fear that this is too forceful and it might drive people away. Meanwhile, the name of God is being erased and replaced with "the universe." So, instead of praying and spending time to build a relationship with Him, people are now trying to "manifest" what they want in life, failing to even question if the things being "manifested" are the will of God.

As you strive to dominate your fear and complete the tasks God has called you to finish, *"Be alert and of sober mind. Your enemy the devil prowls around like a roaring lion looking for someone to devour."* (1 Peter 5:8 - NIV). If you are not careful, you will get so swept up in the things of this world and the new age preaching that you will be employing tactics that will be futile in the destruction of your fears and other struggles because of your inability to clearly target the one behind the schemes.

Ladies with power don't go around condemning people; they simply allow the Holy Spirit to guide them so they can respectfully defend the name of Jesus. The execution of your God-given vision depends on it. The universe cannot help you to dominate your fears, and the enemy knows it. Only the Creator of the universe can do it, and the enemy knows that too. Beware of his schemes.

The enemy gets desperate when He sees God's people getting closer to their purpose. So, when you are close to achieving your goals, he will try everything to stop you. He gets desperate when he sees you close to figuring out who he really is and who you really are. This is the point when you should draw on the power of peace.

If you are going to war for your vision, you have to know what you are up against. The knowledge you receive is not to scare you; it is to better prepare you so you can get the right weapons and do what is necessary to prepare and increase your power.

So, each time the enemy increases the pressure, you need to find ways to increase your power, increase your prayer and ask for more peace and faith. Wear him out with your resilience. You can do it! There is nothing that the devil can throw at you that you cannot handle! Your fears have hindered you for too long, making you unable to do the things you want; the things that will help you to move forward and overcome the defeat and disappointment that you may have experienced in life.

You Have the Power to Rise Up and Show Up

Why should fear get to win? Why should you not be allowed to enjoy your life the way you were meant to? Why should you not be able to access the things that God has for you? You deserve to be free from fear and enjoy a happy life.

Even as you think about stepping out on faith in spite of your fears, be mindful that dominating fear doesn't mean you will never feel afraid again. Oppressors are always out there trying to regain control, so you might still feel a hint of fear whenever you set out to show up. However, when you understand that you were never meant to be a slave to anyone or anything, you will be able to demand your freedom and do anything you can to maintain it. Therefore, when you feel afraid, you will have the courage to proceed according to plan.

When you dominate your fear, you will start to show up differently in every area of your life, and the people who used to push you around are not going to like that. Their success depended on your timidity because that is how they were able to use you. Don't allow the fear of what people think, what they might say about you, or what they might do if you start leveling up, to stop you from going further in your life.

Also, because people may know you from the past and are accustomed to you being a particular way, they might not believe in this new version of you, but that is fine. Pray for them, love them, forgive them and keep moving. The world and everyone else around might not cheer for you, but you have a multitude of heavenly bodies celebrating your pursuit for a life worth living. Focus on that. Focus on growth. Focus on the people around you who are cheering for you.

Girl, focus on the vision.

All About Fear

I've always been a worrier. In fact, I remember being five years old, staying up at night thinking about the well-being of my family members, among other things. The environment in which I grew up did not do much to alleviate these feelings of worry and anxiety, and by the time I got to University, I had the first of many panic attacks, missing two critical exams in the process. Back then, I had absolutely no idea what was going on, which, as you can imagine, made the situation worse, but implementing my own spiritual filtration system was a game-changing decision.

Several events led to my current struggle with fear and anxiety, and even more that prolonged it. There was the time we had to leave home due to threats of upcoming violence in my community and the time my sister and I ended up sleeping on my bedroom floor because shots were being fired in front of our house. There was also a particular day when a group of us had to run to catch a taxi in the midst of shooting while coming home from school and another occasion when we had to walk home from school in order to avoid certain areas because of yet another shooting.

In high school, one of my examinations was interrupted when we had to run from our classroom to the auditorium. We spent the rest of the day crouched under a desk because gunmen had infiltrated the compound, which eventually led to a shootout between them and the police. Even after leaving school and becoming an adult, I still had to deal with situations like this. Once myself and other passengers had to lay on the floor of a bus due to gun violence. There are so many more stories, but I will spare you.

When one goes through life trying to excel and be a meaningful contributor to one's family and society, one doesn't always have the time or wherewithal to stop and contemplate the effects that these events might be having. Suddenly, one day you just wake up and recognize that the things that should be simple are not. The result of these experiences have been social anxiety, a hyper-awareness of my surroundings, constantly scoping the areas for escape points, and briskly walking to my destination. I don't have to tell you how exhausted my body feels after a long day of consistently high levels of adrenaline. I have struggled with anger, irritability, prolonged periods of sadness and, you guessed it, the fear of pursuing my own God-given vision.

This book is about helping you to realize your own power to dominate your fears, so I won't spend too much time talking about my own, but I want you to know that if you struggle with fear and anxiety, you are certainly not alone. According to the World Health Organization, 264 million individuals worldwide have an anxiety disorder, and 4.6 percent of females globally are affected by anxiety.

What I have come to realize is that you cannot fight the power of fear on your own, and pretending that it's not there and that everything is fine will not make it go away. I still experience panic and anxiety attacks; it's still difficult for me to speak to other people. I get extremely startled at the sound of anything that sounds like a gun going off, and there are times when I feel ashamed of feeling this way. However, through spending time with God and allowing Him to reveal His truths, purpose, and vision for my life, I am also confident that I have what it takes to enjoy an abundant life regardless of my emotions.

I know that there is no shame in being imperfect, and I know that with the power that I possess I can live my life the way I want, and so can you. It doesn't matter what caused the fears in the first place; you can dominate them and live the life you want.

Start With the Kingdom

Articulating our struggles with fear can be extremely challenging, but I have found that it's a bit easier when they are first spoken in a quiet space where only the Father can hear. I am not saying you should rule out the idea of seeking counsel from others, but sometimes you will need time to make sense of what is happening so you can put it into words when you are trying to explain it to someone else.

When everything became too much to handle, and when I could not think of anyone to confide in, I started to read the scriptures and pray more than I ever did. Almost everything in my life thus far has been unorthodox, and very often things just don't make much sense.

Focusing on God grounds me. Being able to concentrate on His promises, presence, compassion, and grace has made it tremendously easier to navigate the uncertainties that life brings, and while things are not perfect, I have slowly seen the things that I have dreamed about come to life. When you focus on God, your mind automatically dwell on the things that are good instead of the things that you fear.

You in Mind

While dealing with fear and anxiety, it can be tempting to fixate on needing to show up for other people and look good for the sake of everyone else. All of the changes that you implement should be done because of your need to better yourself and live the way you want, not because you want to be accepted by others. Being a people-pleaser comes from the fear of being rejected, and these unrealistic expectations of having to be liked by everyone will only make things worse.

Be confident in knowing that you don't need to say yes to everyone or everything; know when to rest. Dealing with fear is exhausting, and while you are not going to constantly say no to opportunities because of your fears, you certainly need to be self-aware and know when to regroup, refocus and restart. Don't rush the process; dominating fear takes time.

Unfortunately, fear can cause people to lash out and do things they end up regretting. You don't only have to come to terms with the situations that caused your fears to increase; you also have to reflect on the negative emotions that may have been displayed as a result of them. It is very uncomfortable to think about the part that we might have played in causing a problem to escalate. However, taking responsibility for your actions can be more freeing than you can imagine. This doesn't mean you are going to blame yourself for every bad thing that has ever happened because of your struggles; by assessing your role in the matter, you can learn from your mistakes and implement the strategies that will help to deal with stressful and uncomfortable situations. This can prevent the reoccurrence of negative behaviour.

Identify the Triggers

I had to be honest with myself about the impact that my experiences had on my life, which, let me tell you, was not easy. If you are looking to dominate your own fears so you can start focusing on your vision, you will need to do the same. Identifying the things that caused a significant increase in my heart rate and made me extremely anxious brought feelings of shame, incompetence, and worthlessness, but when I got serious about going after the things that I wanted, it eventually became easier for me to keep moving forward.

If you want to dominate the fear in your life, you have to be able to clearly identify what causes it. From a spiritual standpoint, we know the devil does his part to facilitate fearful situations, but there are other factors involved. What are the specific events and environments that cause you to feel afraid? Are these triggers related to the past, present, or future? Who are the people involved in making you feel afraid? What exactly happens when you encounter these places and these people?

When you are able to recognize what is really going on, it will be easier for you to develop healthy ways to deal with your struggles. You also will learn how to refrain from directing your frustrations toward others around you and focus on the source of your discomfort. You cannot dominate something if you don't acknowledge the hold that it has on you.

Become Self-aware

There are physiological effects of fear; it can affect our breathing, heart rate, and blood flow. Practicing self-awareness is the best way to remain calm when these changes arise. Try writing down the things that your body experiences during moments of fear and anxiety. Don't dismiss your emotions, instead, be mindful of all the changes that occur during each encounter. Calmly allowing yourself to acknowledge the changes taking place will help to lessen the severity and duration of the episode. In order to dominate fear, sometimes you have to face it head-on and learn what it does.

Target the Trigger Not the Fear

Sometimes the enemy uses fear to get us to run away from the very thing that God is calling us to. In my experience, the triggers are not always things that are bad for you. For instance, if you experience fear when taking an examination that you need to pass in order to finish school or if you have a business meeting with potential investors. When you make your preparations, and you are ready to execute your plans, if fear comes creeping in, pray intentionally about the places, people and things that are causing you to feel afraid.

In environments where you fear for your safety, pray for peace and protection. If the thought of taking an exam scares you, take a minute to remind yourself of everything you have studied, and focus on the knowledge that you are well prepared. If you want a raise at work and you are afraid of your manager's response, pray for the right words to say in order to receive a favourable answer. You can also pray that the Lord will intervene and cause him or her to have a great day so that their answer will not be affected by negative emotions. The point is, you can pray for what you want instead of remaining fearful of what could be. **Prayer produces peace, which then creates a clear mind.**

Try making declarations when you pray. Declare that you will walk boldly towards your goals with fear under your feet. When we take this approach and have faith that since we asked this of God, our actions will be blessed, we know that regardless of the outcome, we will be fine; hence, we will no longer fear the results. If your boss says no this time, you can try again because fear did not stop you the last time. Remember, some things require consistent prayer. Don't allow disappointment and the fear of hearing another "no" push you back into the fear zone. This is the time to wield your authority.

Create Bold Goals

We're talking about visualizing your _**highest**_ self! Sometimes fear causes us to get so intimidated that we set goals that are easy; just on the edge of our comfort zone. The things that God wants for us are not mediocre; they are of the highest level. Scripture says that we're the head and not the tail (see Deuteronomy 28:13), a royal priesthood (see 1 Peter 2:9). Our goals should align with the way God sees us and not the way we see ourselves and our situation due to fear. Don't fight the vision that God is trying to place in your mind. It is not a mistake that you want to be an entrepreneur, a doctor, a mother, a writer, a songwriter, a teacher, or a Nobel Prize winner. Your desire for marriage despite the divorce rate in your family is not ridiculous. You can be the first in your family to graduate from university with first-class honours, even if you've passed the age of twenty-five. God wants that for you!

The goals you set for yourself must be in line with your vision. You need to set goals that will challenge you and push you to be more and do more.

Move With Your Thorn

Do it afraid. Choosing to show up doesn't mean showing up only when you think everything is perfect. With that mindset, you will never move from where you are. We all have flaws, and life is not without its prickly problems. Success requires action, and you can achieve your goals regardless of where you were born, how much money you have and how afraid you might feel when you go after it. Don't slip into a cycle of making excuses to stay stuck where you are. Make your plans and take small steps towards making your goals a reality. You don't have to be unafraid to show up. The apostle Paul talked about a thorn that was in his side (see 2 Corinthians 12:7), and while we don't know exactly what he meant, at times fear can seem like a painful, uncomfortable thorn making it difficult for us to do what we want. Paul did not allow that thorn to stop him from carrying out his mission, and neither should you.

Don't Forget the Power That You Possess.

The same power [Spirit] that raised Christ from the dead lives in you.

The Power of Depression

For the weapons of our warfare are not carnal, but mighty through God to the pulling down of strong holds; Casting down imaginations, and every high thing that exalteth itself against the knowledge of God, and bringing into captivity every thought to the obedience of Christ;
2 Corinthians 10:4-5 (KJV)

Our thoughts affect our emotions and our emotions affect the way we act. So then, if our thoughts are negative [fearful] we will be more inclined to act in a negative [fearful] manner. If the enemy can get us to focus on every negative [fearful] thought that comes to our mind, then, ultimately, he will be able to control the way we act or even cause us to not act at all. Fearful thoughts and the subsequent results can create depression. Depression can hinder movement, which means that the main target of this power of the enemy is your preparation process as you move towards your goal.

With depression, the enemy can get you to change the way you view yourself, your situation, and even the way you view God. You might start to think, "How can a God who loves me allow me to be feeling like this? Why is it that even on days that I am surrounded by laugher, I am filled with turmoil?"

It is important to know that if you struggle with depression, it is not an indication that you have failed in your faith-walk, and it is not an indication that God has forgotten about you and no longer loves you.

Intruder Alert

"Finally, brethren, whatsoever things are true, whatsoever things are honest, whatsoever things are just, whatsoever things are pure, whatsoever things are lovely, whatsoever things are of good report; if there be any virtue, and if there be any praise, think on these things." (Philippians 4:8 – KJV).

All thoughts contrary to those that the apostle Paul tells us to focus on are intruders sent by the enemy to distract us from our goals and prevent us from taking the actions needed to attain them.

The word 'think' means to have a particular opinion, belief, or idea about someone or something. To think is to obtain a particular mental attitude by actively directing one's mind to form connected ideas.

Those ideas, beliefs, and opinions that are produced when we think are called thoughts. In other words, the thoughts we have are a result of what we think about. If you think about good things, then you will have good thoughts that will lead to even better thoughts, but if you think about bad things, then your mind will be filled with bad thoughts that may eventually get worse.

On the other hand, there are some thoughts that can suddenly enter the mind without having to think much about them. These are called intrusive thoughts. These are unwanted, unpleasant thoughts or images that can cause distress. These can be thoughts associated with lust, fear, involuntary recaps of painful events that happened in the past, thoughts about doing something awkward or humiliating, and thoughts that cause doubt.

The more severe intrusive thoughts are those related to harming oneself, harming others, or doing something illegal. In any case, intrusive thoughts tend to lead to feelings of guilt, shame, and anger. Depression may increase the likelihood of experiencing intrusive thoughts, and intrusive thoughts might lead to feelings of depression. It is messy, and the enemy loves to keep the people of God trapped in a mess.

When you begin to consistently make use of the powers of God that are available to you, there are a number of mental barriers that are formed to protect your mind. These barriers are there to guard you from negative thoughts that can create a negative mindset and result in negative behaviours. As you get stronger in your faith and start to walk with confidence and authority, the enemy will try everything to push past all your defenses, and he might use negative thoughts to try and get you to question the things you know are true and pure and excellent about God and yourself.

Though these thoughts may breach the barriers, you have the power to push them out. When these unwanted thoughts enter your mind, don't accept them, don't dwell on them, and don't believe them. You'll have to fight to form good thoughts when dealing with depression because the mind will try to lead you more towards the bad ones. When bad thoughts suddenly occur in your mind try not to think about them. Instead, use your mind to actively form positive ideas (thoughts) by thinking about the things that are pleasant. You don't have to prolong every thought that pops into your head.

Training your mind to switch from negative to positive thoughts is not an easy feat, but it is possible. We often try to just ignore these thoughts by pushing them to the back of our minds. This is not healthy and can lead to a serious mental and emotional breakdown. So the goal is not to push these thoughts to the back of your mind but to push them out. In order to do this, you will have to replace the negative with the positive and actively challenge these thoughts as soon as they enter your mind. Pretending that they are not there will only make things worse.

In trying to push them out, ask yourself, "How am I feeling as a result of the thoughts I am having? Will these thoughts help me to execute my vision? What are the fond memories that I can think about to replace the bad ones that keep coming up, and how can I create even more? What does the Word of God say about who I am and what I can do?"

When you are having difficulty trying to find the thoughts that are true, the best place to look is in the Bible. The Word of God is filled with every counter-argument you will need to challenge the negative ideas, so when you cannot think of anything on your own, look there. For every lie that the enemy tells you about your situation, if you search the Bible, you will find the truth. Simply scanning the pages will not help; you have to intentionally make time to study it.

There are a few "I am too" thoughts that tend to pop up whenever we think about changing our life. There is, "I'm too old to do what I want to do now;" "I'm too uneducated to get that promotion;" "I'm too afraid to try again;" or "I'm too inept to start a business."

If you are going to beat depression, intrusive thoughts and all the other negative emotions, you are going to have to replace the words that come after "too" and say:

- I am too blessed to allow the painful past events to dictate my future.
- I am too resourceful to allow a setback to stop my progress.
- I am too creative not to pursue the opportunities that can get me to the next level in my career.
- I am too proud of how far I have come to turn back when I get to a roadblock.
- I am too strong to live my life thinking I am defeated.
- I am too powerful to allow my age to stop me from trying.
- I am too eager for generational kingdom wealth to not prepare for the next level that the Lord is leading me to.

Feel free to write a few of your own:

I am too_____ to_____
I am too_____ to_____
I am too_____ to_____
I am too_____ to_____
I am too_____ to_____

Try to identify the patterns that cause these negative thoughts to happen. Having a journal is a great way to record your intrusive thoughts when they happen and identify the events that happened prior to the thoughts. By identifying the patterns, you will be able to make the necessary adjustments in your routine that might be triggering them. Switching up your routine might help to limit the negative thoughts that enter your mind and prevent you from thinking too much about them. This is also the case with writing them down.

Remember, you cannot always control the thoughts that enter your mind, but it doesn't mean you have to continue to think about them or allow them to control the way you act.

Definitive Power

"Giving thanks unto the Father, which hath made us meet to be partakers of the inheritance of the saints in light: Who hath delivered us from the power of darkness, and hath translated us into the kingdom of his dear Son: In whom we have redemption through his blood, even the forgiveness of sins: Who is the image of the invisible God, the firstborn of every creature: For by him were all things created, that are in heaven, and that are in earth, visible and invisible, whether they be thrones, or dominions, or principalities, or powers: all things were created by him, and for him: And he is before all things, and by him all things consist." (Colossians 1:12-17 – KJV)

The Lord is the Creator of everything that exists on earth and in heaven. As the original Creator, whatever His creations produce technically belongs to Him and can be used or controlled by Him. The enemy is one of God's creations who decided to use what he was given to create forces that he feels will rob us of our vision and lead to our demise.

It doesn't matter what power the enemy creates; there will never be a power that is strong enough to consume or destroy the power of God and any other sub-power of the Holy Spirit. God has the original, all-consuming, final, conclusive, absolute, and irrefutable power, and since that is the power that lives in you, it is within your capacity to overthrow every thought and every evil power that dwells within. It is for this reason you are fully authorized to overthrow the enemy, and it is also the reason he will always be an adversary to the children of God. You are able to do things that he cannot; the very essence of who God is has been embedded within you. Through the power of the Holy Spirit, you can give life to situations. It might take you a while to wrap your head around that but don't take my word for it; you can go straight to the Word of God for yourself.

Do you see why the enemy wants to take you out, and do you see why he uses fear, doubt, and depression to do it? If he can get you to believe the opposite of what God has proclaimed for your life, then you will never use the power that was given to you, which means that he would win. But if you would believe that the negative thoughts you encounter are no match for the peace of God in you, then you would boldly challenge the negative statements that he makes about your identity and your ability to live the life you desire. When the enemy tries to tell you who you are, you need to remind him of who God says you are. Remind him of the power that you possess.

When Pharaoh's sorcerers created the snakes with their staffs, the snake that was created by God devoured all the others. The thoughts that cause you to sink into depression may seem as powerful and as consuming as the truths that come from the Word of God, but all they really are, are cheap tricks. Though they might have some level of power, they are not strong enough to totally consume you and the power that is within you. I know it feels that way when you are in the middle of a battle in your mind. I know it seems as if you are not strong enough to fight back and push them out, and you might feel as if since you have been struggling with this for such a long time, it is too much a part of who you are to be removed without destroying you. However, you can live the life you want despite the struggle.

You can still be the woman you want to be and achieve your goals. Despair is a powerful emotion, but joy is stronger, peace and faith are stronger, and so is the power of prayer and preparation. Don't just concede to defeat; you were born to win. Do the work you need to in order to dominate the destructive thoughts that lead to depression.

Go to therapy if you need to, start to journal or create a fasting and prayer plan dedicated to the demolition of those thoughts; do whatever it takes to find your own *"staff."* The Lord can use anything you pick up to bless you and set you free. It may not look like much in the eyes of others, but once the Lord gets His hands on it, He can transform it into whatever you need to fight the things that are trying to kill your vision.

The power you possess is the definitive, primary, decisive, and dominant power that can override all other secondary forces. The enemy has some power, but he is not all-powerful or all-knowing, and he doesn't have the ability to be everywhere at once. Remind yourself of this daily. Meditate on this fact as often as you can so that when you are exposed to contending thoughts, you'll be able to declare that you have already been delivered from the powers of darkness and you have already inherited the light that can always guide you to freedom.

If you want to show up as the woman in your vision, why not trust the expert who is glorious enough to show up everywhere at once. With the power you possess, the thoughts of suicide, shame, guilt, anxiety, and pain can be demolished. During periods of darkness, you are never alone. In times of turmoil, choose to believe and act according to the power that you possess. When you are being pulled into the dark spaces of your mind, seek the light. Seek out the things that are true and pure and worthy of praise. If you are unable to find anything or anyone else, seek the Lord.

Solitude Scheme

With Kingdom solitude, the Holy Spirit is the one who leads you away so your power may be increased through a period of undisturbed closeness with God. During periods of sadness, the enemy might try to get you alone so he can use your thoughts against you.

When this happens, use his own tactics against him. The next time you are tempted to dwell on negative thoughts during times of solitude, surprise him by reaching for the Word of God. Use your "sword" to destroy every evil thought he sends your way.

Think back on that one thing your therapist said you should do when you come up against these thoughts. Put on your workout clothes and do cardio, start writing a new song or poem, organize a junk drawer, listen to uplifting music, tell God what you are feeling or going through, watch or listen to a sermon or just do whatever you can to fill your mind with good thoughts.

Every time Jesus went into solitude, it was to connect with God and increase His power. When God wanted to steer Jonah in the right direction after he tried running away from the assignment he was given, God brought him to a place of solitude where he had no other choice but to talk to Him. Kingdom solitude sets you back on the course that the Lord has for you, while the solitude that the enemy suggests is to steer you away from it.

When you feel the need to be alone, assess your emotions before committing to the decision. Consider the following:

1. Why do I want to be alone right now?
2. Am I really just depressed and want to dwell on the negative emotions?
3. Do I need to get a bit closer to God today?
4. Do I need to journal in order to process my thoughts?
5. What are the chances of me spiraling into negative thoughts when I am by myself?
6. Do I need to review the plans related to my goals and create some strategies?
7. The things that I want to do during this time of solitude, can I do them with someone else around?
8. Do I feel like God wants to tell me something?

There is power in the pause. Taking part in quiet alone time can help to gain new inspiration, bring revitalization and renew your mind. If the solitude you want came from a place of needing to genuinely work on yourself and lean into the Word of God, then go right ahead.

Even if it is to take a break from the people around you and just process your own emotions, then that is fine too. But the minute you recognize that your thoughts are switching to worry, fear, guilt, anger, and confusion, girl, get out!

The Power of Unforgiveness

"Someone once said that unforgiveness was like a poison you drink while hoping for someone else to die."
— **Jennifer Heng**

Unforgiveness has the potential to create fear to kill our vision, so I am honestly not surprised that this is one of the enemy's opposing powers. We can find so many reasons for the person who wronged us to be the one to ask for forgiveness and a million more as to why we would never forgive them for what they did.

If you are not the one at fault in the situation, and if they are the one who caused the riff in the first place, why should you be the one to be the bigger person? Why should you forgive them after what they did to you?

Well, to put it simply, we're talking about your purpose, vision, and salvation. They may never admit to what they did, they may never see things from your perspective, and they may never apologize, but you have to let go and move on so you can focus your attention on the goals that you have. If the enemy can get you to continuously dwell on all of the hurtful things they did to you, then he would have succeeded in helping you to develop bitterness, hatred, jealousy, and other toxic traits that will eventually lead to toxic behaviours, thus, making sure that you will never be able to show up the way God wants you to.

If you don't move on from what they did, whatever it may be, then you will never be able to walk in the power you were given, and the fear of trusting others will affect your ability to acquire the human resources that you need in your quest to claim your kingdom territories. Also, your mind might be so occupied with thoughts of revenge that you will be oblivious to the fact that the power of unforgiveness is taking over the power of peace. Without peace, there will be confusion, doubt and fear. This means that you will find it difficult to focus on executing your plans.

When you have the power of peace within you, you will be kind to everyone regardless of the things they may have done to hurt you, but where unforgiveness is, so too is the fear of being hurt by others. If this is the case, you could end up treating everyone around you poorly by inadvertently trying to hurt them before they can get a chance to hurt you. On the other hand, you may become aloof in an attempt to protect yourself from what others might do to hurt you.

Choosing to harbour unforgiveness may result in the delay of the things that you prayed for. In this case, it might not even be because God doesn't want to provide them, but because the person who He wants to use to help answer this prayer is the same one you will not even look at.

You have to understand that God is intentional, and so is the enemy. God has seen you achieving your vision, and so has the enemy. While God does His best to help you get to the places you need to go or meet the people you need to meet, the enemy will ensure that the resentment and malice that you have built up grows so strong that you will never even look at the persons attached to your destiny much less speak to them.

Unforgiveness Attacks Your Health

Science has shown that unforgiveness can affect your health by disrupting your brain. This disruption can hinder you from making good decisions. Now, how will you get to that place that God promised you if your decisions are not in alignment with the His plan?

The level of stress that comes from harbouring negative energy towards people can cause tension in your forehead muscle, which leads to headaches and other symptoms such as stomach ache, joint pain, dizziness, and tiredness. Imagine going to the doctor for all of this, and they cannot find an explanation for what is causing the problems in your body. Some people—not you of course—might jump to the conclusion that someone put a curse on them. Jamaicans would say,

"No sah! It look like seh sumaddy obeah mi!" Translation, "Oh my God! I've been cursed."

So they may think it is obeah *(witchcraft),* but all you *(I mean they)* had to do was forgive their coworker for stealing their favorite yogurt from the refrigerator.

What I am trying to say is, all *their* health conditions will make it difficult for *them* to concentrate on the preparations that *they* have to make. So *they* will end up feeling discouraged and overwhelmed and eventually give up on *their* vision. Boy, I really hope *they* can do some internal assessment so *they* don't end up losing *their* Kingdom territories.

Forgiveness is the remedy for all the other negative emotions that it creates. Powerful women forgive not because they always want to, but because they know that unforgiveness pulls them away from their power source. They forgive because they have things to do, and they need every ounce of strength they can get in order to get it done. They forgive because even though they themselves are not perfect, they have received the ultimate forgiveness. They forgive not because they think they are "the bigger person" but because they make mistakes too and will need the power of God to help them on their journey.

You might have been severely hurt by someone you trust. What they did may have caused a lot of damage to your mental stability, level of trust and general way of life. It will not be easy to get over the pain that comes from betrayal, but you have to release the hate, pain, fear of trusting again, and anger so you can receive the power to create the life you have been dreaming about. Do it for yourself.

You cannot afford to lose sleep in this season. You'll need all the rest you can get, and staying up at night because of unforgiveness will only rob you of valuable rest.

Confess and Pray

The Bible is the manual for unforgiveness; that is where you need to start. It is difficult to forgive, but you can try reading/rereading the story of Joseph, and of course, the story of Jesus as a start. This manual can provide you with every detail that you will need in order to start living the life of letting things go. Read it, study it, live it. Here are a few other strategies you can try on your journey to forgiveness.

Just like most of the enemy's powers, unforgiveness works best in the dark. When we're hurt by others, we sometimes keep it locked in our minds, and over time hurt turns to anger and resentment. The first thing you need to do is shed some light on what is happening by finding someone to confide in. The person you choose to confide in must have a proven track record of forgiving others or at least is someone who will listen to what you have to say without judgment. The blind cannot lead the blind, and iron sharpens iron. You cannot seek help from someone who still has not forgiven their sibling for eating the last piece of chicken back in 1971 or is not mature enough to offer sound advice.

You need someone who is going to tell it to you like it is; someone who is going to call you out, lovingly, on what you have been harbouring in your heart and will do so without condemnation. The important part of this step is releasing everything you have been thinking or feeling as a result of unforgiveness, so even if you can find someone who cannot advise you but can only listen, that is a win. If you cannot find someone, then get a book and write everything down, sparing no details. There is also the *Whisper* app that you can download and anonymously write messages.

In order for you to make it past this stage, you need to be completely honest with yourself and the person you are confiding in. Whether you are speaking to someone or writing in your journal, outline everything in detail and be specific about what you feel when you see, hear or think about the person and what they did. You also have to be willing to open up about the hurt you felt when they did what they did.

Say or write the person's name and exactly what they did, and write what you feel when you think about what this person did.

_____
_____
_____
_____
_____
_____
_____
_____
_____
_____
_____
_____

By doing this, the devil is put to shame because you have spoken aloud or brought to life, through writing, all that he was hoping would stay hidden long enough for him to use it to destroy your relationship with God, all your other relationships, your vision and ultimately your salvation.

This process doesn't have to take an hour or a day. Depending on the level of hurt you are feeling, it might take quite a while for you to talk about everything that happened, and that is fine.

Prayer is necessary throughout this process because it will provide the strength you need to touch on uncomfortable subjects. The truth is, sometimes we really don't want to dig up painful events that we bury in our minds. Prayer will provide the courage and help you to bypass your fears as you do it.

Use the power and authority you were given to evict the traces of fear, bitterness, anger, jealousy, and even shame that this unforgiveness might have brought inside you. Use your voice and your words to speak healing and release so you can move on with your life. Use for voice to denounce every plan that the devil has for this power in your life, and ask the Lord to restore every opportunity you missed when you were too focused on what the other person was doing.

Do you realize that even when we say we don't care about the person who we cannot forgive, sometimes we tend to get obsessed with what they are doing? We check their Instagram page just hoping to catch a glimpse of something that will prove that they are not doing well, and if we see that they are doing far better than we expected, we become jealous and envious.

Powerful women cannot show up with jealousy, envy, or bitterness. In fact, if you have been showing up with these things and you think that you are growing and still on the path to your highest self, then you need to pause for a minute and check to see which path you are actually on. I can guarantee that it is not the path that God planned for you.

You need to rid yourself of everything that will cost you your vision. You have worked too hard and made it too far to allow unforgiveness to halt your progress. If your mind is made up and you pull on the power of prayer, everything connected to it will be dominated. Pray for guidance.

You may think that God will be disappointed if you go to Him with this matter, but He will not. He is more likely to be disappointed if you don't do all you can to remove unforgiveness from your heart because then His perfect plan for you will not be achieved.

Not only do you have to pray for yourself, but you also have to pray for them too (see Matthew 5:44). You have to pray that they will be blessed in everything they do. You also need to pray for them to be delivered from whatever caused them to do what they did to you. Pray that they will have the chance to experience the joy of being free from their own fears so they can stop hurting people. It takes a powerful woman to be able to do this. It is a good thing that that is who you are.

Release For Peace

Forgiveness gives rise to freedom, and freedom generates peace. There is an old African proverb that says. "He who angers you controls you." As much as you may think that this person doesn't affect you, let it be clear to you now that if you get angry when you think about the person and what they did, then they have complete control over you, your emotions, and your actions. If your day is ruined when you see them or you lose your appetite–*We love to say this! When that person walks in, we're like "UGH! I've lost my appetite."*–If they get you to put down that delicious and juicy piece of fried chicken that you had your heart set on, then come on, you cannot tell me they have no control over you.

The only person you should surrender control of your life to is God. He should be the one to order your steps and direct your path. If you drop that fried chicken, let it be because you received a conviction from God to be healthier and not because of anger towards someone who probably is on their way to enjoying their own piece of fried chicken.

Do you experience discomfort within you when you are trying to complete your assignment? A feeling of confusion and turmoil? That could be the battle between peace and unforgiveness. You need to let it go. Peace needs to win if you are going to start your business, go to university, or get married. Now, how are you going to marry this man, and you have not gotten rid of the power of unforgiveness that has just been tagging along behind you? Do you think that marriage will fix it? No, ma'am! I can guarantee that the man is going to do things that will just upset your spirit, and you will need to find ways to forgive him in order to make your marriage last.

Release may come when you speak to the person about how you have been feeling as a result of what they did. Before you actually meet with them, you must already have the mindset that you are going to forgive them. You can practice beforehand with your confidant or in your journal and end the session by saying the words *'I forgive you.'* Think about what you will gain after this has been done, and do this as many times as you need in order for it to stick. Remember, there is no light switch that will allow you to switch off your anger. This process is a slow dance between you and God, where you can learn each step, practice each move, and steadily learn your new routine.

You may ask if the person you confided in can be there with you and the other person to act as a mediator, and the other party should also be allowed to invite someone if he or she so desires. Again, when you share, don't hold anything back, but at the same time, don't attend the meeting with the intention of berating the individual. One of the best ways to effectively communicate your feelings without using *blaming language* is to explain using "I" statements. Instead of saying, *"You caused...," "You were so...,"* or *"You didn't have to...."* You can state how the action made you feel by saying, *"When you took my dress, it got ruined, and I was angry and disappointed."* Be clear on the offense that was committed and how you felt as a result of this event without directly attacking the person's character.

Now, remember that this is a conversation, so you will have to be open to hearing what the other person has to say. Just as you might feel that your opinion and feelings matter, then you must also take into consideration that the other party will feel the same. If you want them to value your feelings and opinion, then you have to be open to value theirs as well. This is why it is important to pray and ask God for love and patience before going into this stage because this part will not be easy either.

One of two things can happen after this conversation: the person may apologize for their part in the matter, or they might not. In fact, you may not even make it to this stage at all because the person may not be willing to meet with you out of anger or indifference. If they apologize, then great! Forgive them and move right along with your life. If not, still forgive them and move right along with your life. The objective is to receive peace, and that is whether or not you get that apology.

Forgiveness Reduces Fear

Unforgiveness can produce the fear of trusting others and the fear of life's uncertainties. When you forgive others wholeheartedly, the peace it creates will cause you to recognize your capacity to overcome challenges, which means that you will live a life of freedom to take advantage of every opportunity that comes your way. As you continue to replace unforgiveness with peace, it will eventually become easier to apply this 'release for peace' mindset to every area of your life. Therefore, whenever you encounter a situation that causes stress, as you strive to bring your vision to life, you would have already gained the strategies to release it.

Your thoughts will always be directed towards ways in which you can find peace in your daily life. You'll come to terms with the fact that though people and life are unpredictable and imperfect, negative actions don't have to have a negative impact on your life.

The power of Unforgiveness:

1. Literally makes you sick.
2. Pulls you away from the love of God.
3. Makes you fearful of others.
4. Weakens the power of your prayer.
5. Facilitates the power of hate.
6. Causes internal conflict as peace battles anger and resentment.
7. Prevents you from interacting with the people around you.
8. Makes you skeptical towards others.
9. Causes you to relinquish the control that God should have over your life to someone else.
10. Affects your decisions.
11. Creates toxic traits and characteristics.

Power Lies in the Now

"Forget the former things;
don't dwell on the past.
See, I am doing a new thing!
Now it springs up; do you not perceive it?
I am making a way in the wilderness
and streams in the wasteland."
Isaiah 43:18-19 (NIV)

Claim Your Power

*M*eanwhile, Saul was still breathing out murderous threats against the Lord's disciples. He went to the high priest and asked him for letters to the synagogues in Damascus, so that if he found any there who belonged to the Way, whether men or women, he might take them as prisoners to Jerusalem. As he neared Damascus on his journey, suddenly a light from heaven flashed around him. He fell to the ground and heard a voice say to him, "Saul, Saul, why do you persecute me?" "Who are you, Lord?" Saul asked. "I am Jesus, whom you are persecuting," he replied. "Now get up and go into the city, and you'll be told what you must do." The men traveling with Saul stood there speechless; they heard the sound but did not see anyone. Saul got up from the ground, but when he opened his eyes he could see nothing. So they led him by the hand into Damascus. For three days he was blind, and did not eat or drink anything. In Damascus there was a disciple named Ananias. The Lord called to him in a vision, "Ananias!" "Yes, Lord," he answered. The Lord told him, "Go to the house of Judas on Straight Street and ask for a man from Tarsus named Saul, for he is praying. In a vision he has seen a man named Ananias come and place his hands on him to restore his sight." "Lord," Ananias answered, "I have heard many reports about this man and all the harm he has done to your holy people in Jerusalem. And he has come here with authority from the chief priests to arrest all who call on your name." But the Lord said to Ananias, "Go! This man is my chosen instrument to proclaim my name to the Gentiles and their kings and to the people of Israel. I will show him how much he must suffer for my name." Then Ananias went to the house and entered it. Placing his hands on Saul, he said, "Brother Saul, the Lord—Jesus, who appeared to you on the road as you were coming here—has sent me so that you may see again and be filled with the Holy Spirit." Immediately, something like scales fell from Saul's eyes, and he could see again. He got up and was *baptized, and after taking some food, he regained his strength.* (**Acts 9:1-19 – NIV**).

Sometimes we fear going after our dreams because of the hold our past has on us. We fear being scoffed at by others who knew us in the days when we were not really living at the level that God requires. We also tend to get afraid of making the same mistakes again; getting to the place where we can almost see our vision come to life only to revert to old patterns. We also tend to think sometimes that we cannot come back from our mistakes and that we have wasted too much time to start exactly where we are.

All hope is not lost; it is not over for you. You have not missed your opportunity to release your power, and your vision can still be executed. You can still show up; victory is still a possibility for you. You can still make it to the place you have envisioned for yourself and do the things God has told you He wants you to do. The resources are there; you are strong enough to go on, and you are smart enough; the life you envisioned for yourself is still within reach. You may have messed up in the past, but God wants to start a new thing in you now. God wants to help you to accomplish your vision in this season. He is not concerned with what you may have done in the past. You may make mistakes as you move forward, but you have what it takes to bounce back and keep moving.

All you need to do is claim your power!

Doing the same thing over and over again is not going to get you to your highest place. Making excuses about why you cannot start is not going to make you an expert in your field. You must take action. Feed your hunger for a better life by boldly activating and making use of the power that is within you. Get radical in the pursuit of your purpose.

Fear will always try to get you to quit, but you can push it out and set your plans into motion regardless.

You can still claim your power. The Holy Spirit is still available to you. You may feel as if you have lost your way because of fear, or you may feel like you no longer have the strength the go on because of depression, unforgiveness, anxiety, insecurity, self-hate, addiction, guilt, or shame, but be reminded that you can still gain access to the things that God has prepared for you. Once you allow the Holy Spirit to do His job, then you will be able to regain your strength. The things that have been causing you stress will fade away, and you will be able to continue on your journey.

Maybe you are angry at God for the struggles that you faced, and maybe you are not. You may have given up on life entirely because of the hardship you have faced, and maybe you are close to giving up on God and your vision entirely, but let this be your season of trying one last time. In this season, try to do everything you can to use the power you were given. Allow God to place you on a new course, and try not to look back at where you came from.

To wrap up our discussion on getting to the highest possible level in your life, here are the 4 *Ds* that will help you to dominate your fears, execute your vision and show up as the powerful, war-winning woman you were created to be.

1. Decide

I was listening to a podcast the other day, and the guest they had on said something that had me questioning my own attitude towards failure. He said if you take away the money and assets that Bill Gates and Elon Musk possess today, there is a good chance that in the next couple of years, they would have regained all they had lost, plus maybe even more because of the mindset these guys have developed. Instead of choosing to dwell on their situation and what they lost, these men would do everything they could to get back to where they were in life, if not further.

The position you find yourself in a few years from now will depend on what you decide to do **now**. Do you want to go through life wondering what would happen if you take the first step regardless of your fears, or will you decide to actually make a move? You serve a God who is capable of providing all you will need to make your dreams a reality. You have to make a conscious decision to utilize the power you possess to drive out the powers of the enemy and secure the life you want. Consider the following as you make your decision:

1. What are your current goals?
2. Are they goals that will get you to your highest place, or are they limited because of fear?
3. If you know you are not where you want to be physically, financially, mentally, emotionally and spiritually, are you willing and ready to spend the time to develop a plan that will get you to where you want to be or will you spend the rest of your time perpetually trapped in the visualization stage?
4. Will you start to develop a prayer routine?
5. Will you find ways to live peacefully?
6. Are you going to let go of the people who hurt you?
7. Will you find ways to fight negative thoughts?
8. Will you ask God to help you?

The Lord is waiting for you to decide. He wants to move in your life. God wants to help you execute your vision, but you have to decide to do what is required of you. Will you decide to spend more time cultivating your power through prayer? Will you begin to prepare for the things that He is calling you to?

When you choose the things of God and fill your life with His power, there will be no room left for any other power. The enemy will try to get his powers into your space, but God's presence will render it full to capacity.

2. Discredit

*"There is **now** therefore no condemnation to them which are in Christ Jesus, who walk not after the flesh, but after the Spirit." (Romans 8:1 – NIV – emphasis mine).*

"The voice spoke to him a second time, "Don't call anything impure that God has made clean." (Acts 10:15 - NIV).

The negative things that the enemy has led you to believe are false. In order to actively discredit his allegations, you will need to know the truth of God. In order to find out what the Lord really thinks about you and discover how you can be the woman you want to be, you have to connect with Him through prayer, and you have to feed your mind by reading the Bible daily.

We're often reluctant to connect with God because of sin, past mistakes caused by disobedience, and the way we see ourselves as a result of the things we may have done in the past. Our fears can be so consuming at times that they distract us from the things that will bring us joy and peace. Once we decide to ask God to forgive and restore everything that disobedience took from us, then it will be so. Once we actively train our minds to push past fear and seek the things that are true, we will gradually develop a strategy for discrediting the lies of the enemy.

Differentiating between condemnation and conviction is not easy. When we read the Word and hear the plethora of things we should not be doing, it can feel as though we're facing constant disapproval. The enemy is the one who reminds us about the mistakes we have made when we try to move forward. He will tell you that God can never love you because of how you are or what you have done. He will have you believe that God requires perfection. He might flood your mind with thoughts such as, "You'll never be the woman you want to be; you are not a good Christian because of the things you are struggling with; or you don't deserve to be happy." These are all lies!

When the Holy Spirit convicts, it is more of a nudge, prompting you to think twice before doing something. He shows us how happy we can be when we abide by the instructions of God and how these instructions protect us. He lovingly reminds us of who we are and encourages us to choose the right course. Conviction is about showing us that we are not necessarily doing what is right; the Holy Spirit will never associate our sin/struggle or fears with our identity.

Let's try writing out a few positive "I AM" affirmations without writing the negative words that the enemy uses. For example, instead of "I am not worthless." write "I am valuable."

I AM_____

I AM_____

I AM_____

I AM_____

I AM_____

Write as many as you would like, keep them wherever you would like, and refer to them as many times as you need. There is no shame in having to remind yourself of who you are, and doing this every day will make it easier for you to shut down the lies of the enemy.

Remember, when Jesus was fasting in the desert, and the devil came up trying to twist the words of the Bible, He was able to discredit every last one because of what He knew to be true, and He knew these things to be true because of the connection He had with God. Get connected. It is through knowing who God is and who He says you are that you will be able to push past all fear and execute your vision.

3. **Deviate**

To deviate is to depart from an established course or from the usual/accepted standards. If you recognize that the current course you are on is not working for you, then you need to change your course regardless of fear. If you realize that the guidelines you have been operating with are no longer serving you, then it might be time to pivot.

Our lives are made up of daily routines and these routines dictate whether or not we fulfill our goals. These routines can also be responsible for the level of fear we encounter on a daily basis. In order to change the course of your life, you may need to assess your routine to determine if it consists of tasks that will make you successful. If not, you may need to make the necessary adjustments. For instance, you cannot pray and ask God to help you to reach your goals and then spend most of the time watching Netflix and scrolling on social media. You'll need to find the right balance between work [preparation] and play.

Change takes time, and sometimes there are so many things we want to change that we get confused and overwhelmed. Commit to the deviation process for thirty days and choose one area of your life that you want to see transformed. It could be losing weight, doing a social media detox to work on your plans, or eating healthy. Maybe you can actively try replacing negative thoughts with positive ones, read the Word, or spend time in prayer. Whatever it is, write it down and be specific. Instead of writing "I will focus on losing weight," say "I will give up eating out, and I will not eat after 6 pm." If it is engaging in Kingdom solitude during the time you would be watching Netflix, make a note of exactly what you will be doing instead; it could be reading the New Testament chapters or journaling and praying about a specific topic.

You may need to get a separate journal, but here is an activity to start with:

For the next thirty days I will focus on:
_____
_____
_____

Think about a reward for hitting the halfway mark:
_____
_____
_____

Start a journal. Write down everything, and be sure to speak positively to yourself at the end of each day.

Depending on the goal, you may want to identify someone you trust and ask them to pray for you during this time.

My power partner is:
_____

Change takes time, so be patient with yourself, but remember, change also takes discipline so know when to get back on track and continue the process.

4. **Dominate**

The grace of God is renewed every morning. Despite what happens in life, we have the opportunity to access His power every day.

Expect challenges, sorrow, and unexpected outcomes. It is a part of life, and it is unavoidable. Just know that for every obstacle you face in life, there are solutions.

For the changes you will be implementing, make a list of possible obstacles and write the corresponding counteraction that you will take if/when they arise.

Obstacles

1. _____
   _____
2. _____
   _____
3. _____
   _____

Power Moves

1. _____
   _____
2. _____
   _____
3. _____
   _____

When these obstacles come up, don't stop! If you miss a day because of events out of your control, start fresh the next day and add an extra day to the thirty. If you had to skip day ten, your day ten would now be what would have been day eleven. The goal is to ensure you get thirty days regardless of obstacles. Though you strive to do thirty consecutive days, this may not always be possible. However, you still need to focus on developing the habits of commitment, pivoting, determination and discipline. So, strive to achieve thirty days even if it is not thirty consecutive days.

You can reinvent yourself if you want to. You have the power to create and execute new habits and routines that are aligned with the current vision you have for your life. Despite what you may have believed, choose now to believe that you deserve what you desire.

With the limitless power of God that lives within you, you can dominate your fears and all other powers of the enemy. The same power that raised Christ from the dead can help you to execute your vision.

The time to start executing your vision is **_NOW!_**

Ephesians 3:20-21
"Now unto him that is able to do exceeding abundantly above all that we ask or think, according to the power that worketh in us, Unto him be glory in the church by Christ Jesus throughout all ages, world without end. Amen." (KJV).

Notes

The Vessel of Power

1. Romans 8:11
2. John 10:10
3. Matthew 10:1
4. Acts 2
5. 1 Corinthians 12
6. Kevin Downswell – "Carry Me"
7. Romans 8:38-39

Purposed for Power

1. Romans 8:30
2. Colossians 3:12
3. Romans 8:17
4. Isaiah 43:4
5. John 14:12-14
6. Luke 22:44
7. Esther 4:16
8. Philippians 1:6
9. Genesis 3:15

The Power of God

1. Exodus 3:13-17
2. Exodus 14:10-14
3. Exodus 16:1-3

4. Exodus 13:17-20
5. Exodus 7:10-12
6. 1 John 4:1
7. Psalm 84:11

The Power of Peace

1. John 14:27
2. Judges 6:23
3. Philippians 4:6-7
4. Ephesians 5
5. 1 Peter 3
6. 1 Timothy 5:8
7. Romans 14:12

The Power of Prayer

1. Philippians 4:6-7
2. Luke 10:19
3. Romans 8:26
4. 2 Corinthians 7:14
5. Matthew 18:20
6. Matthew 9:17-18
7. Matthew 9:25-29
8. James 4:7

The Power of Faith

1. Mark 5:34
2. Mark 5:35-42

The Power of Preparation

1. 2 Corinthians 10:4-5

2. Ephesians 6:10-18
3. Matthew 25:1-13
4. Matthew 7:24-27
5. Ephesians 6:12

The Power of Fear

1. 1 Peter 5:8
2. 2 Corinthians 12:7

The Power of Depression

1. 2 Corinthians 4-5
2. Philippians 4:8
3. Colossians 1:12-17

The Power of Unforgiveness

1. Matthew 22:37-38
2. John 13:34
3. Matthew 5:44

Power Lies in the Now

1. Isaiah 43:18-20
2. Acts 9:9-19
3. Joshua 24:15
4. Romans 8:1
5. Acts 10:15

About the Author

The power of God that raised Christ from the dead can be activated within every woman, transform her life, overpower her fears and help her to create and live the life of her dreams.

As a writer, empowerment speaker, mentor, and Bible teacher, Okema Watson has made it her mission to share this message with every woman on earth. She strives to share everything that she has learned about tapping into the power of the Holy Spirit and boldly challenging the enemy in order to live a life of abundance.

Okema holds a BSc. in Psychology and Management Studies, and works as a Human Resource Manager on the beautiful, blessed island of Jamaica.

www.ingramcontent.com/pod-product-compliance
Lightning Source LLC
Chambersburg PA
CBHW070540170426
43200CB00011B/2494